No Challenge

No Change

Growing Up Black

In

New Mexico

Charles E. Becknell, Sr

Jubilee Publications

Edited by Candy Hibben

Library of Congress

Control Number: 2004092488

ISBN 0-9744573-0-2

Printed in the United States of America by

Morris Publishing

3212 East Highway 30

Kearney, NE 68847

1-800-650-7888

Acknowledgements

To Dr. Tobias Duran, the Director of the Center for Regional Studies at the University of New Mexico, whose assistance and encouragement made this publication possible. Also, to my wife Pamela – thank you for your love, support and understanding. To my son Charles - thank you for the research on the Becknell family.

Dedication

This book is dedicated to all of the brave soldiers who have challenged racism and made life better for all of us. Because of you, I realize that peace and justice is still possible.

Table of Contents

Introduction

The decision to write this book evolved over several years. One reason for my hesitation is that I consider myself to be a very private person. I realized that even though I had once been a public figure, I guarded my privacy to the point that when I felt my privacy being invaded, I became very defensive. However, with this book, my privacy is not being invaded; I am inviting others into my private world. I consider this to be a big risk, and I have long felt that it takes a great deal of boldness, or even arrogance, to write about one's own life. How does one "tell it like it is" and expose some of your innermost thoughts, feelings and experiences? Writing about the victories and triumphs come easy, but what about the failures and the mistakes that sometimes lead to embarrassments? How does one strike a balance and "let the chips fall where they may?" I have asked myself these questions for a couple of years. After much soul searching I decided to take the risk and publish *No Challenge, No Change.*

Now, I have come to the conclusion, with a great deal of guidance from the Holy Spirit, that this book is not a story of my life, for I have not done any great thing that would deem me worthy to be recognized in this manner. This book is designed to open up a window for others to look into and see what it was like growing up black in an atmosphere of racism and segregation in southeastern New Mexico. This is not an easy story to tell because not all memories are good, yet, the good ones are those that we readily remember. We tend to suppress memories that are painful. We bury them and go about our business for years, until something happens that causes those unpleasant memories to resurface. When we are children and we are exposed to hurts, pains and other unpleasant or painful experiences, and we have no one to explain what is happening, those things don't go away – they are usually suppressed. We grow up and we outgrow many of the unpleasant experiences, but we do not outgrow the suppressed feelings caused by those unpleasant experiences. They remain with us mainly because they were not brought to closure. Racism is a dehumanizing, cruel and unpleasant experience. My childhood was in part shaped and defined by the racial atmosphere that existed in our country at that time. How I saw the world, and how I tried to make sense of that world as I grew into adulthood, would be defined by my childhood experiences while growing up in Hobbs, New Mexico.

My childhood years helped shape my personality and my character. I thank God that I had Ebenezer Baptist Church in my life. In addition to my mother, Ebenezer helped to keep the unpleasant experiences in balance. In such an adverse racial environment, it was the church that taught me when to challenge, how to challenge, but most of all, how to survive by trusting God. It was at Ebenezer that I first heard the encouraging voices of challenge and change that stirred up something in me that slowly continued to build up over the years. Those voices of change spoke softly through my Sunday School classes, through my BYPU (Baptist Young People's Union) training, and through sermons that were preached by my pastor, Reverend F. W. Wells. I was taught that God is not pleased with things the way they were. We were reminded that the way things were was not the way God intended for things to be. We were encouraged to follow God's plan and then we would be on the road to eliminating racism in our society. In numerous sermons I heard that God's people must be His agents for change and if we don't challenge the system, there will be no change. If we don't challenge the system, most people, black and white, will feel as though the way things are is the way things are supposed to be. Even though I heard those messages about challenge and change as a child, the fire of activism did not really ignite until right after college.

This book will relate more to the experiences I have had rather than to the things I have accomplished. Race and race relations will be the central themes of this work. For it has been race, race relations, education, religion, family and obstacles that have shaped who I am today. Furthermore, what has affected me as an African American has affected hundreds of others as they have moved through life struggling with some of the same issues. As I move through life's experiences, there will be more to say and more to do. God is not through with me yet and I am still a work in progress. When God gets through with me the final chapter can be written; probably by someone else.

In February, 1965, I moved to Los Angeles, California, to attend graduate school at Pepperdine University. I went to California to seek opportunities that I knew were not available to me in New Mexico. At that time, if there was one person who was a prime candidate to become a conservative Republican, it was Charles Becknell. I earnestly believed that people were poor, not because of race but because they were lazy and did not work hard enough. I believed that all people were the same and if you went to school, prepared yourself and worked hard society would be fair and treat you fairly. I also believed that the American dream was equally available to all. To say the least, I was very conservative in my thinking and in my expectations.

Then an event occurred that changed my life forever. In August of 1965, the Watts riots erupted. This was a tragic occurrence and it caused me to look seriously at the economic and social disparity between blacks and whites; the *haves* and the *have nots*.

The whole concept of *privilege* began to surface and influence my way of thinking. Some people never think of the word *privilege* and many are in denial regarding this social and economic advantage for white people. Some of the big advantages were that whites could choose where they wanted to live, they could choose the schools they wanted to attend and where they wanted to sit on the bus, and they had institutions that backed up their choices. Whites could choose the restaurants they wanted to dine in and could stake them out for themselves by excluding others. They had the absolute authority to do so. I learned at that point that *privilege* means to be comfortable in your surroundings and have the power and authority to protect that comfortable environment. This reinforced the notion of *haves* and *have nots* and made it painfully clear at that time that there was a *place* for whites and a *place* for blacks. As long as everyone stayed in their *place*, everything was fine. Problems would occur when blacks attempted to come out of their *place*.

Also, in 1965, I was fortunate to be selected for the Sears Company Management Trainee Program in Long Beach, California. Five people were selected and I was the only African American in the group. I worked hard, (I believed that this would make me stand out), and I put more into the effort than was expected (as I was taught) and I excelled above the others. When the program was completed, the four white trainees were given the choice departments to run and I was given the least productive one, in terms of commission overrides. I decided that hard work was not the main criteria for advancement – it was about race. After a year in California, I moved back to New Mexico and began to teach school. This was one of the best decisions I have ever made.

As I reflected on those flames of activism that continued to well up inside of me, I remember a workshop for teachers that I attended in 1968, sponsored by the University of New Mexico. The theme of the workshop dealt with cultural awareness in education. Throughout the morning I heard references being made to the "three cultures of New Mexico"; that New Mexico is a tri-cultural state and how we needed to enhance educational opportunities for these "three cultures."

I looked around the room and I saw Hispanics, Anglos, Native Americans, African Americans, Jews, Italians and a few other cultures. My immediate thought was *Somebody is being left out and I need to find out who and why.*

"Excuse me, I have a question."

"State your name, position and your question."

"Charles Becknell, teacher, Albuquerque Public Schools. My question is, to which three cultures are you referring?"

The response was, "The Anglo, Hispanic and Native Americans."

"Sir, I have been in New Mexico all my life. I know of many other African Americans that were here before me. Are we not worthy of recognition? Do we not possess a culture that should be included?"

The response that came from the workshop presenter was, "Oh, no, you have not been excluded. We see African Americans as part of the Anglo culture."

My eyes were opened and my life was changed. I became angry, hurt and confused. I then went on a mission to ensure that New Mexico would never be referred to as a tri-cultural state again and that not only would my people, but all people, be seen as a part of the cultural mosaic of New Mexico. I wanted to work toward never having a child of any culture wonder, *Am I in or out?* When we exclude, we isolate. When we exclude, we assume an arrogance that can lead to the assumption of superiority. We also create a class of people who are culturally lost and struggle in a forest of bewilderment trying to find who they are and where they fit in society.

Racism can wear many masks, because racism has many faces. Racism goes beyond dislike. It even moves beyond hatred. Dislike and hatred by themselves, without the power or authority to act, can be benign. When racism is backed up with power and authority, we find segregated and unequal schools, lack of equal employment opportunities, and the *haves* and *have nots*.

Growing up in Hobbs, New Mexico in the '40s, '50s and the front end of the '60s has given me a unique experience, an experience shared by very few people. I *lived* the '40s and '50s. I experienced the limitations and the degradation of segregation. I felt the uncertainty and uneasiness of integration. I observed, lived and participated in civil rights activities, and I navigated the minefields of *equal opportunities* that I was told I had access to. I worked for three governors; only one earned my respect. This book is based on my own observations and experiences. As you read it, you may reject what I have to say. You may not agree with the conclusions I have reached or the assumptions that I make, but all I ask is that you respect my right to say what I think and feel. We may have traveled down different roads and along the way have seen and interpreted things in different ways. But when all is said and done, we are all God's children and we should all be trying to get to the same place – a place where race, ethnicity, color, gender or physical limitations will not matter.

Someone said, once the mind is expanded to the dimension of new thought, it never returns to its original form. I hope this work expands your thinking about race and race relations in New Mexico. We all search for that place where peace prevails and all people can live with dignity and respect. My prayer is that we will continue to search for that special place.

How Did I End Up in New Mexico?

The Becknells and New Mexico

I have always wondered about my family history. I had done bits and pieces of research, but had never gotten very far. It was a big surprise to me when I found out that I was not the first Becknell who had come to New Mexico.

During the summer of 1988, I received a phone call from one of my cousins, Theodist Lewis, who resides in Kansas City, Missouri. Little did I know that this phone conversation would change forever how I felt about myself and being an African American in New Mexico. My cousin informed me of the need to have a Becknell family meeting because there were some critical issues that needed to be discussed regarding our family background. Theodist had been conducting preliminary research on the Becknell family history also and he discovered that our family is directly connected to William Becknell, founder of the Santa Fe Trail.

I said to my cousin, "Wasn't he a white guy?"

His reply was in the affirmative. He also said that his preliminary research, which included a great deal of oral history and exploring records from Red River County, Texas, led him to strongly believe that, in spite of William Becknell's race, there is a connection. I had always been interested in tracing my family history. That phone call became the impetus for me to begin my research, and my family history began to unfold.

In 1817, William Becknell married Mary Cribbs in St. Charles County, Missouri, and the couple had three children – William, John and Cornelia. Missouri did not begin keeping marriage records until 1850, so I do not have in my possession an official marriage record. However, all other historical accounts refer to Mary Cribbs as the wife of William Becknell. Oral family history says that she was of African descent.

In the fall of 1835, after a successful career of merchandising generated by the opening of the Santa Fe Trail in 1821, William Becknell, his wife Mary and their three mulatto children moved to Red River County, Texas. In 1836, he was elected to the House of Representatives. After a recount, it was determined that Collin McKinney was the winner and William Becknell was forced to relinquish his seat. It has been suggested that the reason for the recount was related to Becknell's benevolent attitude toward slavery and his relationship with his slaves.

African Americans in the territory of Texas were by no means considered equal to whites, and they enjoyed very few rights. Equally, many people of mixed race were denied the recognition of kinship and the financial gain that they should have inherited. Such was not the case with William Becknell's family. According to physical descriptions of his family members, his children and grandchildren were considered mulatto. Census records strongly imply what other records do not implicitly state, that many of the people who held the Becknell name and lived on Becknell property were descendents of William Becknell, Father of the Santa Fe Trail.

Oral family history further tells us that Mary Becknell would send William and his two sons to Missouri on a periodic basis to buy her family out of slavery. Little by little, more and more of Mary's African American slave relatives would be brought to Red River County to live with the Becknell family. According to Mary Becknell's last will and testament, she wished that the "Negroes would be treated kindly after her death." Is it ironic that slaves would be referred to as "Negroes" who are "to be treated kindly" prior to and during the Civil War?

All of the Becknell's mulatto slaves and family members lived on the same property, cohabited, reproduced and continued to multiply in numbers and recognition as a family. The Becknell offspring became known as walking contradictions; they were symbols of conflict between Southerners' ideology of race and family. Typically, in slave and slave-owner relationships the conflict was present when children were denied or when affection toward them was acknowledged. According to the law, there was no relationship between the slave owner and the children that he had born with a slave. Any relationship with a white parent was simply erased. There could be no attachments to or claims made on the white family unit.

This was not the case with William Becknell. While the law did not acknowledge the mulattos of the society, William Becknell's relationship with his wife, mulatto children, grandchildren and slaves was a testament to the prevalence of relationships between blacks and whites. Although the situation was common, in most cases it was difficult and often impossible to establish the identity of the white parents of slave children.

When I started this research, I was aware of only a few resources available that would uncover my family's history. Few of the resources proposed a strategy that would guide me through the maze of dead ends and other pitfalls that I encountered, especially when researching the pre-Civil War era. I soon began to realize that the years 1865 to 1870 were the most pivotal because during this time the Civil War ended and the slaves were emancipated. The 1870 Federal Census was the first nationwide census after the war, and the first to name the recently freed slaves. This census became an interesting and important tool for determining the makeup of the Becknell ancestral family.

My research has determined the timeline of the Becknell family was as follows:

- 1817 William Becknell married Mary Cribbs in St. Charles County, Missouri. The couple had three children – William Alexander, John and Cornelia.

- 1821 Mexico won independence from Spain and William Becknell opened the Santa Fe Trail, making three trips between 1821 and 1824. It is logical to believe that if a man owned five slaves he would not leave them home as he embarked on the most difficult journey of his life. Did he cook his own food, wash his own clothes or feed his own animals? Or did he take people along to perform these duties?

- 1830 The Saline County, Missouri slave records indicate that William and Mary Becknell owned at least five slaves. The question that again begs to be answered is did he take slaves with him on his Santa Fe Trail expeditions? If so, their place in this historic journey should be recognized.

- 1835 William Becknell and "family" moved from Missouri to Red River County, Texas. The "black Becknells" all originated in Clarksville, Texas, which is in Red River County. Oral history also tells us that there were white and black Becknells in the same town, but due to social separation, they conducted themselves as though they were not related. One of my aunts related that the white Becknells did look out for the welfare of the black Becknells by providing food and hand-me-down clothes on occasion.

- William Becknell was given government land grants in Red River County in exchange for his military service and assistance in developing what is known today as the state of Texas.

- Coupled with the land he purchased, William Becknell amassed over 5,000 acres of Texas land, a bridge spanning the Sulphur River, the town of Bagwell, Texas, including the graveyard, livery stables, grocery stores, schools and the church. Becknell owned everything from Red River to Sulphur Bottom (approximately 45 miles). During his time of fame and prosperity, Becknell was a slave owner. Issues of concern from the white society included his attitude toward slavery and how he treated his slaves as family (many were) and shared his property with them. Again, oral history tells us that black Becknells inhabited the town of Bagwell, Texas. William Becknell had given the land to them. Several years ago, my cousin Theodist went to the Red

River County Courthouse to look up documents so we could reassert our claim to the land. He was told by the clerk to come back after lunch. When he returned, he was told that the records could not be found because they had been destroyed in a fire a few years before.

- 1858 Prior to his death, William Becknell passed on the entire estate, including the land known as the Becknell Survey and five slaves, to his wife Mary Becknell. The total estate was valued at $13,000.00.

- 1862 In Mary Becknell's last will and testament she appointed Benjamin Epperson as the executor of her estate to divide the property among her children and relatives upon her death. Among the property listed are four slaves. Of particular interest is a male slave named Harvey Becknell, who is believed to be the grandson of William Becknell through his son, John.

- 1863 While on her sick bed, Mary Becknell married a white man, John K. Rodgers, a long time business associate of William Becknell. Census and slave records identify her as Mary Rodgers.

- After Mary Becknell died John Rodgers inherited the Becknell estate. Shortly after, he married into the Lennox family. Later, the Lennox family became executors of the estate and acquired all of the land designated for the black Becknells.

- 1870 Red River County census records identify a young mulatto male named Harvey Becknell, Jr. He was the son of the aforementioned slave, Harvey Becknell, Sr. Oral family history says that Harvey, Jr. was the great grandson of William Becknell. Harvey, Jr. is also referred to as "Hobb" by African American Becknells and in a death record.

- 1871 Suit #3912 was filed by Martin and Phyllis Becknell, former slaves and family members of Mary Becknell. The suit is filed to reclaim the Becknell estate, and distribute the property among the African American descendants of William Becknell. That suit was lost, but many in the Becknell family feel that there is still a claim to be made.

- Harvey Becknell, Jr. married an African American woman named Malinda. They had six children, two of whom were Lindsey and George. George's death record identifies Harvey Becknell, Jr. as "Hobb" (referred to earlier).

- Lindsey Becknell married Iceola Young and they had 10 children, one of whom was Cullen Becknell.

- 1941 Cullen Becknell and Zelma Dobbins had a child in Levelland, Texas and they named him Charles Becknell (the author).

- 1942 Zelma Dobbins and her two children moved to Hobbs, New Mexico.

- Charles Becknell marries Mary Katherine and they have three children, Desiree, Valerie and Charles, Jr.

Chapter I

The Torn Page

I don't remember much about my life before the age of six, but my birth certificate indicates that I was born in Levelland, Texas, on June 22, 1941. I was delivered by a midwife – at that time, most African Americans did not have access to doctors and hospitals. To lie in a hospital bed next to a white person meant that you were their equal. Even if one had the money, the situation would have been no different.

My mother moved to Hobbs, in southeastern New Mexico, when I was 18 months old. I understand that she had a hard time providing for my older sister and me. At that time employment opportunities in Hobbs were limited for African Americans. Until the early '60s jobs for African Americans were limited to maintenance men, domestic workers and yardmen. Picking and chopping cotton provided seasonal work but offered limited career opportunities.

I do vaguely remember my maternal grandfather, whom I called "Papa." He took me everywhere he went and I remember holding his hand as we walked. My father was off fighting in a war and after "Papa" died, I remember looking down this one dusty road (Midwest Street) in Hobbs hoping to see my father walking down the street. I looked for a man in a uniform, with stripes on his shoulders and medals on his chest. He never came for me! After the war, he went his way and my mom went her way. Probably one of the greatest destructions of war is not the devastation of countries, but the devastation of families.

Growing up as a black child in Hobbs, New Mexico, was a truly unique experience. Even though Hobbs is located in New Mexico, it is more Texan and southern in its characteristics. Hobbs is not on a major thoroughfare; consequently, contact with outside ideas was limited, especially in the pre-television era. The influx of new ideas was slow to come.

When did I first realize that I was black and different? It is difficult to say. I knew at an early age that something was going on. I never saw any white kids at school. I thought that maybe the first realization was when I heard the word "nigger," but the first time I heard that word was not from a white person, but from someone black. Maybe it was when I looked around my community and saw only people who looked like me. Maybe it was then that I realized that I was different. The question that often came up in my mind was, *Why are we here and they are over there*?

There is nothing wrong with being different, however, I grew up with the assumption that to be black and different was to be inferior. I also grew up believing that to be black was a badge of dishonor and that equaled second-class citizenship. Second-class citizenship meant that you were to say *Yes sir* and *No sir* to white males, regardless of their age. Another rule that I learned at an early age was that blacks had to remove their cap or hat in the presence of a white person. Black men and boys, regardless of age, were frequently referred to as *boy*. (Facial hair on a black male was unacceptable because hair was symbolic of masculinity.) It was told to us that in some areas of the South, facial hair could get a black man lynched.

I learned to fear white policemen at an early age. I believe that this was one of the survival techniques instilled in us by our parents. This fear was reinforced when I was around 10 years of age. Someone came by the house and said that one of my uncles, Robert Baker, more affectionately known as "Bo Peep," had been beaten almost to death by the Texas Highway Patrol on the outskirts of Andrews, Texas. His only crime was being black and refusing to say *Sir* to white police officers. This taught me that police officers were to be feared. This is a latent fear that many

African Americans carry around today. White kids were taught to respect police. Black kids were taught to fear police and not to antagonize them in any way.

I grew up with the cruel racist antics of Amos and Andy, who initially were white men impersonating black men on the radio. They amused other white people by reinforcing stereotypes, which further projected the idea that blacks were second-class citizens to be laughed at and ridiculed. I grew up with the image of Stepin Fetchit, who was projected as the slow moving, head scratching, slow thinking, shuffling *Negro*This is the way many whites saw blacks at that time.

Being black and different also meant that you were to enter a white person's house through the rear, never through the front door. There were places that we knew we were not allowed to go and if we did, there were rules that had to be followed. Even in death, the rules of segregation had to be adhered to. In Hobbs, blacks and whites were not allowed to be buried in the same cemetery; there was a white cemetery and a black cemetery. However, in death, blacks and whites have something in common; they are equal because they are both dead. I wondered if the white people in Hobbs felt that heaven would be divided into sections, one for blacks and one for whites?

The negative impact of racism, separation and rejection could be seen in the actions of those blacks who bleached their skin in efforts to have light skin like white people. Some blacks used harsh chemicals on their hair to take the kinks out, to straighten the hair so it would hang down like white people's hair. Many blacks were told not to drink coffee because it was thought to make the skin darker, and the darker the skin, the harsher the treatment from white society.

Until 1954, the school system and the communities in Hobbs were totally segregated; blacks lived in one section of town and whites lived in all the others. When I entered the public schools, the Hobbs School Board implemented a policy stating that black children who came into the system at the age of six had to come in as "pre-primary" students. Blacks called this "pre-primmer." This meant that children at the age of six could not enter the first grade until they spent a year in "pre-primmer." This only applied to black children; consequently, many students in my age group, myself included, did not enter the first grade until the age of seven. They eliminated that policy at the end of that year. This meant that children coming in the following year entered into the first grade along with "pre-primmer" students. What a tragedy! Students who were a year younger, from the same family, entered school with their older brothers and sisters, and eventually graduated at the same time. Apparently, we were held back due to some social experiment performed by the Hobbs School Board. I am not sure why that practice was stopped, but my class was held back a year for no other reason except the color of our skin, and probably negative assumptions about our intellectual capacity.

I recall the all-black school I attended, Booker T. Washington; all grades attended this one school. Elementary and junior high students were on the same grounds with high school students.

Some of the classrooms were old military barracks. The principal was black, my teachers were black and all the students were black. The only time I saw a white person is when we went to "town" or worked on someone's yard. My first grade teacher was Ms. Porter. I remember that Ms. Porter always smelled fresh in the morning and that she was a patient, caring and resourceful teacher. I fell in love with my first grade teacher!

During the first week of school, each student was given a book, *Dick and Jane.* I could not relate to very much in that book. My step-dad did not look like the father in the book. My step-dad went to work with coveralls on, not a double-breasted suit. He had a garden tool in his hand, not a briefcase. We had no white picket fences in front of our house; for a while, we had no fences at all. The only integrated symbol in the book was that dog, Spot!

Spot was black and white. We didn't have the other things that Dick and Jane had, but we did have a dog!

I vividly remember that when I received my first-grade book, one of the pages was torn.

I asked Ms. Porter, "Why is my book torn?"

She replied, "These books are sent to us after the white children finish with them."

The African American children were given used books! When the white kids got new books, we got their leftovers. Some of the books even had missing pages! Consequently, the title of this chapter, "The Torn Page," came from that experience.

This event came to mind about seven years ago, I was undergoing training to teach a course on diversity in the workplace. One of the workshop activities required us to write down our first experience with bias or prejudice. I reflected for a moment and I remembered inquiring about the torn page in my book and how the question, *Why*? has been on my mind ever since. Each *why* leaves a scar. Racial scars cut deep and bleed profusely. Although the bleeding eventually stops, the scars remain as reminders of the pain. At some point you learn to move on, try to ignore those scars, but each act of racism creates a new scar, and unfortunately the old ones remain.

We hear that we should get over these scars. We can get past stretch marks; they don't cut, they just stretch the skin, such as when someone calls you a name, someone slights you by delaying service in a restaurant because of your color, or a taxi driver looks at you and keeps on driving. You say a few choice words and complain to the manager or hail the next cab. Those are stretch marks. Scars involve being turned down for a job or promotion because of the color of your skin, and you and everyone else knows that you are the best qualified. Or when lay-offs occur and you are handed the first pink slip. Or when you are turned down for an apartment rental by being told that the place was just rented, only to have a white friend check later and be told the apartment is still available and for them to come by and pick up the keys. If you have experienced scars attributed to racism, you always remember even the smallest ones, or something happens that reminds you that the scars are there and they are brought to the surface over and over again.

The torn page was the first of many scars that I would experience. I assume that growing up in Hobbs was not the best place in New Mexico to grow up, but similar conditions existed in Clovis, Roswell, Carlsbad and Artesia. We had no paved streets and we had no sidewalks. The skating rink and the swimming pool were off limits. As a result, I never learned to skate or swim. The only way we could eat in a restaurant was to go around back where a table was set up in the kitchen specifically for blacks. There were separate water fountains for blacks and whites, as well as separate bathrooms, and signs were placed in plain view to enforce the separation.

During my sophomore year in high school, I attended a varsity football game in Kermit, Texas. Segregation was very much alive, consequently, there was a section for whites to sit and another section for blacks. The section for blacks was marked with a sign that read "colored." A rope divided the two sections. Two gentlemen from Hobbs, one black and one white, attended the game together. They were co-workers and good friends. Since they could not sit in the same section, they sat next to each other and carried on their conversation over a rope! They sat shoulder-to-shoulder, shared opinions about the game and cheered for the Hobbs Eagles in spite of that symbolic rope.

In the all-black school that I attended, before our school day began we had prayer and when it ended we prayed again. We also said the Pledge of Allegiance to the flag everyday. In spite of segregation, we pledged loyalty to the country that divided us by race and excluded us by law.

Every person I saw in my classroom was black, except for George Washington and Abraham Lincoln hanging on the wall. My favorite teachers were my first grade teacher, Ms. Porter and my second grade teacher, Ms. Valley, whom I also had again in the fifth grade. My band teacher was Mr. Murphy, an excellent teacher and a very patient man. At Booker T. Washington School, corporal punishment was an acceptable and well-used practice. Almost every teacher had a belt and would use it immediately upon any infraction of school rules. Disruptions, speaking out of turn, fighting, being late for class or even not knowing your times tables could lead to punishment.

The principal of our school was a man we secretly, but affectionately, called "Skull." There is a difference of opinion among many former students as to how Principal Ralph Littleton got the nickname "Skull." My interpretation is that since Mr. Littleton was such a strict disciplinarian, I equated going into his office with the skull and crossbones on a bottle of poison. That meant death! Figuratively speaking, that's what happened to you when you were called into his office. There was always a possibility that you would not come out alive! We feared "Skull" because we respected him. This fear was also an acknowledgement of his authority.

At Booker T. Washington, we had teachers who cared about our education and they insisted that we learn. Emphasis was placed on the basics: reading, writing and arithmetic. No one left Booker T. Washington without knowing how to read. Our teachers lived in the community. They did not come to the school and teach their class, and then after school, drive across town to a home in another community. We did not only see them at school, but in church and at community activities. They were truly a part of our community.

Unfortunately segregation was a way of life in Hobbs. Although we didn't like it, we did accept it. It was not economically safe to protest, make waves or even question segregation. If a young person stepped outside the rules, parents were held accountable, and if they wanted to keep their jobs, they had better keep their children in line.

Booker T. Washington School had no cafeteria; therefore hot meals were not available. Most of the children had to either bring lunch or go home. My mother would sometimes place a sausage patty between a biscuit for me, and off to school I went. Now, a sausage biscuit appears to be a modern invention. I often wonder where McDonald's got the idea. I came to the conclusion that he called my mom and she told him how to do it!

Black children from Tatum, Lovington and Eunice, New Mexico were bused to Hobbs to attend Booker T. Washington. Some lived only a few blocks from the school in their community. I suspect that the bus passed by the white school that black tax dollars helped support, to get to a black school that received very little support. The children from Tatum had to get up at 4:30 to 5:00 a.m. in order to catch the bus to Hobbs. There were only a few students to be picked up. The bus stopped in Lovington, picked up more black students and proceeded to Hobbs. These students started the process over the next day. This madness continued until the school year of 1954. I assume that this practice was very costly, but it was a price that officials were willing to pay to preserve a segregated way of life. I might also add, a very expensive way of life.

The students who were bused could not participate in after school activities, because the bus left for Tatum at 4:00 p.m. If they did participate, their parents would have to drive from Tatum to Hobbs to pick them up. Racism is not only ludicrous, it is costly. For years that bus ran from Tatum to Hobbs and back, like a slave ship carrying its cargo to and fro.

Booker T. Washington School did have football and basketball teams. The football players had to be rough and tough because the practice field was dirt with small rocks and weeds. Booker T.

Washington played other segregated teams from surrounding Texas towns – La Mesa, Midland and Odessa. Many of the young men who were bused were excellent athletes and would have helped Hobbs High School teams immensely, but were unable to play because of their race. Both programs were hurt as a result of segregation. I am not sure where the equipment and uniforms came from. I would assume that they were hand-me-downs also. I looked up to those players on the Booker T. Washington Tigers. Players such as Aaron Williams, Curtis Battles, Charles Mitchell and Londell Butler, to name a few, were my heroes and my role models.

Up until the early or mid '40s there was an air base in Hobbs. Black service men would come into the community to the "Black USO." Here they could socialize, write letters home or simply relax. I suppose that there was also a whiteUSO in the white community. When the base closed, the USO building was turned into a recreational center for young people in the community. It became known as the "Center." This was probably the best thing to happen to the black kids in Hobbs. This was a place where we could go and "hang out," listen and dance to the latest music, eat hamburgers, meet friends and shoot pool. The white kids had always had their places to go and we were not allowed. The Center was *our* place. It became the focal point for social activities in the black community.

The black adults had their place to go also. It was called the "Sunshine Club," named after a gentleman called "Sunshine" Butler, the owner and proprietor. Again, blacks could not patronize the bars uptown, so Mr. Butler opened an establishment that lured some of the up and coming black artists to Hobbs. These people later became well-known performers. Many black artists were touring on what was called the "Chittlin' Circuit." This was a string of black nightclubs throughout the south where black artists would play and move on to the next town. I remember Little Anthony and the Imperials, Fats Domino, Bobby Blue Bland and James Brown coming to Hobbs, to name a few. On one occasion, Fats Domino came to Hobbs and performed at the Sunshine Club. After the performance he had to leave town because he and his band could not find a motel in Hobbs that would rent to them because of their skin color.

Hobbs was also, at one time, home to a black semi-pro baseball team. The players had to rent rooms in existing homes because housing was limited in the black community, and whites would not rent to blacks. Those were the rules, and believe me, there are some who live by these rules even today, not only in Hobbs, but also in other cities in New Mexico. Roswell also had a black semi-pro team. One of the players Willie Stargell, who went on to play in the major leagues, has often talked about his experiences in Roswell, New Mexico.

The black community in Hobbs was pretty close knit. An African proverb says, *It takes a village to raise a child.* The black community in Hobbs was a village because people looked out for each other's children. They truly believed in what the Bible taught, *Train up a child in the way he should go and when he is old he will not depart from it.* Discipline, even corporal punishment, could come from other community members. They, in turn, informed your parents and you received the discipline again. I use the word discipline here as a polite term for *whupping.* Some people say whipping, but if you ever got a *whupping* you know the difference. The Bible tells us to *spare the rod and spoil the child.* In those days, the rod was not spared, neither was the belt, tree limb or any other weapon of mass destruction that our parents could get their hands on.

There is a song that says, *the night has a thousand eyes.* So did the black community in Hobbs. It seemed as though everyone was watching. As kids, we could not get into mischief because eyes that you never knew were watching woulds ee you doing something out of the ordinary, and report you to your parents. Once I was driving down Main Street and a girl I wanted to talk to was going in the opposite direction. I blew my horn; she stopped and I made a U-turn in the middle of the street. When my step-dad got home he said to me, *Why did you make that U-*

turn on Main Street? Someone saw me, reported me and I got busted and was duly punished.

I learned at an early age that it does not matter whether you are a child or an adult, you cannot get away with anything and it not be discovered by someone. It may take years but eventually things will catch up with you, usually at an inappropriate time. It is best to get potential trouble out of the way early. Delayed trouble is usually the worst trouble you can have because when it comes it is unexpected. And hits you like a ton of bricks.

When my mother married my step-dad, I was seven or eight years old. My life changed forever. Although the relationship between my step-dad and me changed for the better when I was in junior high school, my early years were filled with fear. I really never had a childhood. I remember crying a lot, being punished a lot and feeling alone a lot. When my sister Betty got married and left home, I felt that my world had ended. She was my best friend. Now she was gone and I was alone. At least she was free, but I wondered, *How long Lord? How long will I have to suffer the pain of being punished so often? Why, O Lord, why?* I never knew when, and often I never knew why. I had no one to protect me. I had nowhere to go, so I grew up in a vacuum; in fear and feeling all alone.

I seldom had the opportunity to play with other kids, except at school. When I was young, I had sandy red hair, so the other kids used to tease me and call me "Red." I would be walking home and some of the kids would shoot me with BB guns. They would hide behind trees and bushes where I could not see them, and I would feel the sting of BB pellets on my legs and back. The scars brought on by ridicule and ostracism probably hurt the most. Many times I felt like an outcast among my own people.

Although Hobbs was a segregated community, the first real friend I had was a white kid named John Goddard. John's parents were some of the finest people I ever met. They accepted me in their home – *through the front door*. John and I played together, and we had our secret hideouts where we would eat potato chips, drink sodas and eat candy bars. I don't really remember how I met the Goddards, but I do know that God sends special people into your life at a time when they are needed the most. John and I went to the same junior high school and our paths crossed several times, but our individual interests pulled us in different directions. There will always be a bond of friendship between us.

I can always remember having jobs to do. I had weeds to chop, lawns to mow, hogs to slop, dishes to wash and chickens and dogs to feed. As a caddy, I shagged golf balls and carried golf bags for the rich and elite at the Hobbs Country Club. I could not use the bathroom at the Country Club because that was against the rules (whites only). Consequently, I had to walk about 200 yards from the caddy shack to an open ditch and that is where I would relieve myself. I had to bring my own toilet paper with me from home.

Since I was not old enough to drive at the time, I had to walk approximately five miles to the Country Club and five miles back home. A couple of years ago, my good friend, Tony Knott, Chief of the Hobbs Police Department, invited me to go to a luncheon with him at the Hobbs Country Club. I thought for a moment, *There was a time when I could not enter this building.* I went to the luncheon with Chief Knott and smiled as I entered. Although I didn't really need to, I used the bathroom! At least for the Hobbs Country Club, the question *How long, O Lord, how long?* had been answered in my mind.

During my early childhood, we lived in a house on East Skelly Street. We had no indoor bathroom or running water. Saturday night was *bath* night. Water was heated in a pot and poured into this galvanized tub. The tub was quite small, but you found a way to bathe. The other days you washed yourself with a *wash rag* from water in a *wash pan.* We relieved ourselves in a *slop jar*, which was a big pot that had a lid on it. The *slop jar* was an essential item to have because if the weather was bad, you didn't have to take that long walk to the outhouse. A Sears catalog was also a most prized commodity. Since we could not afford toilet tissue, pages from the Sears catalog worked just fine.

My mother was, and still is, a very religious person. I grew up in the church and was required to attend service every Sunday and all other church activities. Mom always prepared for church on Saturday. On Saturday the Sunday meal was cooked, shoes were shined and clothes were ironed. No work was to be done on Sunday. Going to church or not was never an option. It was mandatory in our household. It is still mandatory today. If you reside in Mom's house, even if it's a short visit, church on Sunday morning is mandatory. No excuses!

I was baptized at the age of 12, during the month of April and the weather was still very cold. We did not have a place inside the church to baptize, so we had to drive out to a pond where cattle came to drink. I remember praying for sunshine all morning. It never came and I felt like a popsicle after the baptism, but it is a day that I will always remember. Reverend F. W. Wells, the pastor of Ebenezer Baptist Church, baptized me. He served as the pastor of that church for 62 years. Reverend Wells was a remarkable man who was not only my pastor, but my friend, mentor and spiritual adviser until the day he died. There will never be another like him. He was a leader and on the forefront of racial change in the Hobbs community.

Chapter II

Separate But Unequal

Prior to 1954, separate but equal was the law of the land. However, separate was never equal. Black schools did not receive funding equal to white schools. Black teachers were not paid the same as white teachers. Facilities and supplies in black schools were woefully lagging behind white schools. The signs of separation were evident everyplace. Black and whites could not drink from the same water fountains, eat in the same restaurants or use the same bathrooms. Blacks could not rent hotel rooms. They had to sit in a designated section in movie theaters and in the back of public transportation. White barbers would not cut a black man's hair. This is the atmosphere that was prevalent in my community while growing up in New Mexico.

We can trace the pattern of separate schools in New Mexico back to 1923. In an act of the New Mexico Legislature [which was amended in 1925] provisions were made for the optional establishment of separate schools for African American students. It stated that the schools were to be as well kept, functional and efficient as those schools provided for whites. There were nine segregated schools located in Roswell, Artesia, Carlsbad, Hobbs, Tucumcari, Las Cruces, Vado and Alamogordo. These schools were located in seven counties: Chavez, Eddy, Lea, Curry, Quay, Dona Ana and Otero. In 1947, the Legislature of the State of New Mexico appropriated $35,000 for a survey of schools for recommendations for improvements. This survey included segregated schools, and it was hoped that the findings would be disclosed to the public. However, this did not happen.

In 1949, a group of concerned citizens, sponsored by the NAACP Albuquerque Branch and the Albuquerque Civil Rights Committee, undertook the task to discuss and report on the shameful conditions of this separate system. From the investigation that was conducted and the research analyzed, a complete picture could not be formed but did bring the problem to light. It is believed that a more thorough study would have revealed a more deplorable situation. The report, *New Mexico Segregated Schools: A Survey,* written by Frances Salisbury, Prentice Hapgood and Madison Strait, admitted to being very conservative in the presentation of outrageous facts. The facts that were reported about six school systems in New Mexico are reprinted here.

Roswell

Carver School had an average daily attendance of 90 students that shared five classrooms. There were four teachers that provided instruction for grades one through twelve in what was described as an "old physical plant with cement floors and a new addition with tile floors." The school was located near the river and the environment was extremely dusty with heavy traffic and no zoning signs to slow down speeding motorists. The seating consisted of outdated stationary desks, and the classrooms had inadequate lighting. The auditorium was an assembly space created by the opening of folding doors between classrooms.

The school was listed as having modern sanitation facilities but not satisfactorily maintained. Of important note were the safety conditions. The classrooms were identified as having adequate fire extinguishers, but desks blocked the exits, and leaking gas was found in the shower rooms.

Biology and chemistry were taught every other year by rotation. The outdated science apparatus depended on a water supply that had to be brought in through a window by a hose.

Artesia

The Carver School in the Artesia School System consisted of one teacher who had the first three grades with 20 students in all. Short class periods existed for fourth, fifth and sixth grades, utilizing combination grade teaching. There were two separate buildings with inferior equipment supplied for both. The investigation by the NAACP discovered that the primary room consisted of seats and chairs that were too large for the students. Sadly, there was no playground equipment furnished by the School Board.

Carlsbad

The Carver School in Carlsbad was located and constructed in such a way that presented a safety hazard. There were deficient library facilities and the school lacked the resources to support a competitive athletic schedule because of its size. Part of the African American population of Carlsbad lived in the downtown area and the others lived around the school. School attendance for African Americans was difficult and expensive. A transportation cost of $2 a month had to be paid by the downtown students who were not fortunate enough to ride the public school bus.

The narrow halls of the school were a death trap if fire should ever ravish the building. When open, the classroom doors extended almost across the hall and effectively divided it into compartments. It is hard to imagine small children in a panic pushing on both sides of one of these doors in a desperate effort to escape. The Carver School was poverty stricken and lacked reading rooms to encourage students to take advantage of the limited offerings of the library.

Hobbs

Booker T. Washington School averaged approximately 247 students. Nine teachers taught first through twelfth grades in eight classrooms. The school was located in the African American section of town and had no paved walkways. The school buildings were not permanent constructions. They were used barracks that could not be expected to last an extended length of time. The building furnishings were considered modern, and the teachers were well qualified to provide the students the best education possible, in spite of being overloaded. The Commercial Department was considered too small to take care of interested students, and the instructors had to divide their time between first grade and the Commercial classes. The Home Economics Department had a good foundation but was also considered too small to offer the full opportunity for students.

Clovis

The Lincoln-Jackson School was moved to a new location in 1949. However, some of the buildings from the old location were also moved. To complete the new setup, some buildings were brought from a flooded-out junior high school to the new location; the white school received a new brick building. Sanitation and safety in this school were identified as being deplorable with improperly kept restrooms, floors and arrangement of furniture. In fact, the report stated that they found a dead cat in one of the rooms, and the principal confessed that he did not know how long the animal had been dead. Furthermore, the doors opened the opposite way and had faulty locks. It is stated that the principal was opposed to a curriculum of manual training but wanted to establish training in mechanics and cosmetology. The report indicated that he had the highest regard for the School Board and Superintendent for granting all of his requests.

Las Cruces

Booker T. Washington School in Las Cruces was published as being one of the better segregated schools, along with the Booker T. Washington School in Hobbs. This is attributed largely because of excellent parent teacher cooperation and aggressiveness. However, they still could not be compared with white schools. To equalize the shortages called for large and expensive expenditures. The students needed more space than was available. Unlike the other segregated schools, there was a widespread belief on the part of whites and African Americans in Las Cruces that at least the high school should be integrated.

Many tax dollars went toward the maintenance of a dual educational system. With the exception of Hobbs and Las Cruces, many of the segregated schools consisted of tarpaper and board barracks hauled away from flooded areas or abandoned army camps. New Mexico housed the most modern scientific laboratories in the world yet failed to provide black students with a science program. Sportsmanship and competition were absent during the early days of school segregation because there were no substantial athletic programs. Schools with good sports and academic programs existed in towns where white children lived and went to school, but African Americans were unable to enjoy the same benefits.

So, we see evidence that the schools in New Mexico had been a part of this *separate but equal* practice. However, in 1954 the Supreme Court of the United States handed down a landmark decision in the case of *Brown vs. Board of Education.* The Supreme Court mandated that schools desegregate "with all deliberate speed," requiring "good faith compliance at the earliest practical date." State-sanctioned racial discrimination was ruled unconstitutional under the equal protection clause of the Fourteenth Amendment of the U.S. Constitution.

Prior to the *Brown vs. Board of Education* Supreme Court decision, the only southeastern New Mexican cities that still had segregation in all of their schools were Clovis, Hobbs and Lovington. Other schools in the southern New Mexico area still had segregation only in the elementary schools. In my opinion, many school boards felt that they had complied with the Supreme Court's ruling by retaining segregation on the elementary level and desegregating on the secondary level.

The state NAACP challenged this practice of integrating on the secondary level and remaining segregated on the elementary level on the grounds that Carlsbad still maintained a segregated system and had not complied with the Supreme Court's ruling. The NAACP had received a complaint from a black parent stating that since she had to take her child across town to a black school, passing white schools along the way, this amounted to a segregated system. The Carlsbad school district countered by saying that since they had integrated the secondary level, the charges brought by the NAACP were not valid.

The NAACP again pointed out that integration only occurred on the high school level. Under constant pressure by the NAACP, on July 9, 1954, Superintendent Tom Hansen admitted that segregation still existed in the elementary grades in the Carlsbad Public Schools. At the same time he stated that "non-segregation had been a long-range policy of the Carlsbad Board of Education, a voluntary program that had been planned many years ago." He also stated that at that time "plans were about three-quarters completed."

On July 12, 1954 the Artesia Public School System abolished school segregation. The public school staff was also integrated. It is difficult to substantiate how many black teachers were not assigned to any school and were forced to seek employment elsewhere. Hobbs was the last school district in New Mexico to end segregation in its schools.

New Mexico was the site of a study in the early '50s conducted by the Ford Foundation Fund for the Advancement of Education. The survey was under the supervision of Margaret W. Ryan. Her survey included communities in New Jersey, Ohio, Illinois, Indiana, Arizona and New Mexico. These states were chosen because their constitutions left the issue of segregation or desegregation up to local school boards.

Margaret Ryan revealed that prior to the Supreme Court decision requiring desegregation in all public schools, 17 states allowed their schools to remain segregated: New Mexico and Arizona were among these 17 states. Her task was to learn what methods school administrators used in the process of desegregation, what segments of the community favored the move, what groups opposed it and the results in each community. Her surveys were conducted in Hobbs, Carlsbad, Clovis, Las Cruces, Alamogordo and Roswell, New Mexico. Margaret Ryan's findings can be found in the publication *The Negro of the Schools* by Harry S. Ashmore, University of North Carolina Press, Chapel Hill, 1954 (Second Edition).

On July 12, 1954, the Hobbs Board of Education met to hear requests to suspend a motion that would end segregation in its school system. Spokesman for the group was Reverend Bill Carter, head of the Segregation Committee and pastor of Rock Chapel Church in Hobbs.

The group charged that undue haste had been used in the Board's decision to abide by the Supreme Court decision and that the Board should suspend its earlier decision. Attorney C.M. Neal supported this statement by indicating that only three states had been involved in the Supreme Court decision, and New Mexico was not affected since the State Attorney General had declined to be a party as a "friend of the court." Reverend Carter stated that regardless of the Supreme Court, the decision to end segregation was against the "law of the Bible." He further stated that the "law of the Bible" was the one the entire nation should abide by. Key words in the Supreme Court mandate that gave many school districts an excuse to stall on integration were "deliberate speed" and "compliance at the earliest practical date." Ignored in the mandate were statements such as "separate educational facilities are inherently unequal."

In their attempt to maintain segregation in the Hobbs Public Schools, on July 23, 1954, the Segregation Committee handed down a resolution that advocated that a black person run for the School Board in order that he may secure equal facilities for the segregated schools. (This was a direct attempt to return Hobbs to the *Plessey vs. Ferguson* doctrine, "separate but equal.") This petition had more than 2,000 signatures of people who felt that the schools should have separate but equal facilities. The resolution stated:

> "We the Segregation Committee wish to inform you, the colored people, that we do advocate segregation; however, we also advocate equal rights for you and your children. So, let's work

> together to get a member of your race on the Board so that you may receive equal rights."

By the following day, the Segregation Committee had more than 6,000 signatures on a petition to return the Hobbs schools to segregation. The Segregation Committee had very little support from the black community. However, there were some key black leaders who did support the committee's proposal.

During the period from July 24 to August 8, 1954, the situation in Hobbs was extremely tense. A direct physical confrontation seemed inevitable. The Segregation Committee applied constant pressure to the School Board. On August 8, 1954, the Hobbs Board of Education relaxed its prior ruling on segregation and stated that grade school pupils could attend any school in the district. The only restriction imposed was that the parents had to make a formal request, which the Board could either accept or reject. Students attending school out of their districts would be required to furnish their own transportation and these students would be subject to transference if a school became overcrowded. To put it mildly, this was a proposed compromise with the Segregation Committee.

The Segregation Committee, unwilling to compromise, called a general meeting that, ironically, was held at Hobbs High School.

At this meeting the committee gave the School Board an ultimatum to comply with its resolution returning Hobbs schools to segregation by August 28, 1954. Reverend Carter threatened to step down as moderator of the Segregation Committee because he felt that a riot was inevitable and said, "I feel that a preacher has no right to lead beyond failure of a peaceful settlement of any community problem." He warned that there was a possibility that parents would boycott the school, and further warned, "This town is going to explode into riots." After this statement some members withdrew from his church. This showed the depth and intensity of the race problem in southeastern New Mexico. Then Reverend Carter decided to stay on as moderator. When it appeared that integration was inevitable, he urged his people to be peaceful.

On August 30, 1954 Hobbs, the last public school district in the State of New Mexico to end segregation, opened without incident and very few absentees. (The above information concerning Reverend Carter and the Segregation Committee was taken from excerpts printed in the *Hobbs Daily News-Sun.*)

The battle for equal education then moved into the classroom, and this has been proven to be the toughest battle that black people have had to fight in the educational arena. The fight of the black child in the integrated classroom has been for survival.

Prior to 1954, many white classroom teachers had definite negative attitudes regarding black children. These were usually based on attitudes reflected by society as a whole. Even though the schools were integrated, what went on inside the classroom remained unchanged. Nothing was changed in regard to teacher attitudes, teaching and testing methods. The system was unchanged and uncommitted to equal education. There were a few black students who competed and survived in the integrated classroom, but there were also probably twice as many victims.

Chapter III

A Different World

When the school doors opened in the fall of 1954, the Supreme Court had spoken and Lea County listened. Black kids and white kids in Hobbs walked into a new era in race relations. For five or six hours a day, two races that had previously been separated now played sports and sat in the cafeteria and classrooms together. Our world would be vastly different than the segregated world we knew before. There was apprehension and anxiety on both sides. As African Americans, we did not know what to expect or how we would be treated. Would there be hostility? Name-calling? Fights? These questions would be answered on the first day of school.

I lived about two blocks short of the boundary line that would allow me to ride the school bus. On the walk to school, we had to walk through a white neighborhood. With the exception of a few people who drove by and yelled out "nigger," we had very few problems. Those who rode the bus experienced more difficulties because for the first few weeks hostile white students yelled "nigger, go back where you came from, we don't want you here," and a few obscenities when they got off the bus at the school. What really stood out in this situation was that the teachers and administrators stood by and did nothing! They did not try to admonish these white students. There was no counseling or any other kind of intervention. I quickly came to the conclusion that some of the teachers and administrators did not want us there either. The law of the land had thrust us all into a situation where none of us wanted to be. As black students we had to enter a semi-hostile environment, outside of our own neighborhood and the tension could be felt from day one. We were not wanted and we knew it.

When the schools integrated, I entered Heizer Junior High School. Heizer was a new school and we were the first students to attend. Along with the taunting that took place when the black students got off the bus, there were a number of incidents that occurred that still continue to be brought to my remembrance. I was walking down a hallway one morning and three white boys began to taunt me. One said, "Where are you going nigger boy?" Another pushed me and blocked my pathway. I grabbed him and took him to the floor. While I held him down, the other two began to kick me, but I held on to the one I had down. One teacher came out and it appeared to me that he took forever to pull those students off me. I was taken to the office and was told to "grab my ankles." This meant to bend over so that I could receive smacks on the butt with a paddle from the principal. (Corporal punishment was legal at that time.) The white boys were sent back to class and that was the end of the matter for them. One of the most prevalent complaints that I heard, observed and continue to hear, even to this day, is about the unequal punishment exhibited on the part of school officials; black kids feel that they receive more severe punishment than white kids do. I believe that if statistics were ever kept, this would prove factual.

The principal of Heizer Junior High School was Ray Wasson. The nickname given to him by the students was "Ironsides." He had gray sideburns and I believe that is how he got that nickname. He was not known for fairness when it came to black students. When a black student went into his office, the student came out holding his butt. When a white child came out, the child usually had gotten a stern lecture. I spent three years at Heizer trying to avoid ending up in the office of "Ironsides."

The next event I recall that made an impression on my life occurred in the eighth grade. The English teacher asked the students to write a book report on any topic of their choice. She suggested that we write about our summer vacation, but she left it open. Since I did not know what a vacation was, I could not relate to that topic. I remembered that a white man and his wife had given my dad a lot of books and magazines because they were moving to another city. My dad had the books stored in a small storage house that we had in our backyard. One day, while rummaging through these materials, I discovered a set of books by William Shakespeare. I perused each book, but *Midsummer Night's Dream* caught my interest. I decided to write on what I learned from this book.

A week before the report was due, the teacher asked each student what he or she was going to write about. As she went around the room, the responses from the white kids centered on vacations, trips or their pets. I could not wait until she got to me. When my turn came, I blurted out "Shakespeare's *Midsummer Night's Dream."* She looked stunned, then responded with a sarcastic "Oh no. You people are not ready for that yet." I remember that statement as if it happened yesterday. Although I can't remember what I eventually wrote my report on, I do remember the feeling I had as a result of her statement. I am not sure if her statement was directed to me as an eighth grader or as a black person. Either way, she should have been more encouraging.

During my three years at Heizer Junior High School, I was involved in several extracurricular activities. I played clarinet in the school band, and I played in both the concert band and the marching band. My band teacher, Mr. Hatch, was a nice man. He was a very pleasant and fair person. I also played football, basketball and ran track.

When I entered junior high school and up until the time I graduated from high school, I did not have one black teacher. In fact, there was only one black teacher, Mr. Lyle Collins, at Heizer and none at Hobbs High School.

I was fortunate to have a basketball coach who brought me out of my shell. I was shy and introverted and I did not trust many white people, or in fact, many adults. Consequently, I kept a lot of things inside. But Coach Jim McPherson had the ability to draw the best out of me. I took a strong interest in basketball because of him. It was Coach McPherson who also encouraged me to run track.

Furthermore, during my years at Heizer I had a ninth grade English teacher named Mrs. Jernigan. Mrs. Jernigan was a strict, no-nonsense teacher and she never smiled. One day a student informed us that Mrs. Jernigan was smiling in the classroom. This would have been a truly historic moment and we did not want to miss it. We ran to peek in the room to capture this rare occasion. By the time we arrived, we were disappointed; Mrs. Jernigan was not smiling. We all ran when she stared at us over her glasses.

As a teacher, Mrs. Jernigan pushed us, she challenged us and in her own way, she encouraged us. At the time, I did not like Mrs. Jernigan very much. I though she was mean, not just to me, but to all students. I could not wait to graduate from Heizer and go into high school.

When graduation day came, the only thought I had was that now I am free from Mrs. Jernigan. When I got to high school, I received my class schedule and I saw the name "Jernigan" as my tenth grade English teacher. I thought, God is surely punishing me for some reason – another year of Mrs. Jernigan. Now I looked forward to the eleventh grade. Then I could get Mrs. Jernigan out of my life forever. When I entered college and took freshman English, I did so well in the class that my teacher, Dr. Davis, asked me where I had gone to school. I told him I had graduated from Hobbs High School. He said I was head and shoulders above the other students in his class. A light bulb went off. I said, *Thank you, Mrs. Jernigan. I didn't understand you then, but I thank you now.*

When I entered Hobbs High School, I left behind a perfect attendance record at Heizer. I loved school and I had not missed *one* day. In spite of having to take Mrs. Jernigan's class again, I had perfect attendance during my sophomore year. One day during my junior year, three of my friends and I decided to play hooky. I don't know what motivated us to do this because there was nothing to do in Hobbs. We rode around for a while, taking side streets to avoid detection from our parents and other *spies* in our community who would report us to our parents. The pool hall opened up in the afternoon. Little did we know, but the school had called our parents and reported us absent. I had never been absent before, so I did not know how the system worked. I thought I could miss a day and my parents would never know. I was about to shoot the eight ball into the side pocket when someone said, "Here comes Tommie Lee." Tommie Lee was my step-dad. We all ran out the side door of the pool hall, because we *all* knew that trouble was about to enter the room. We scattered in different directions.

I spent hours hiding out, but I eventually got hungry and it began to get cold. I knew that eventually I would have to face the music, so I went home. My parents didn't say anything. I had convinced myself that as soon as I walked through the door the roof was going to come down on my head. I entered the house and nothing happened. I got a little nervous at this point; all sorts of ideas began to go through my mind. Did they know? Was Tommie Lee's coming to the pool hall a coincidence? (At this point I did not know that the school had called.) One thing I was convinced of was that if they did know, they would not let it pass. I ate dinner. Nothing was said. I washed the dishes and did my homework. Nothing was said. I watched TV for a while; still nothing. At this point, I felt like inviting them to get it over with. I was now convinced I would pay the price when I went to bed. I put on some sweatpants and a sweatshirt under my pajamas and an extra shirt under my sweatshirt. I waited and waited and nothing happened. I finally fell asleep. About 5 o'clock in the morning my step-dad woke me up and told me to get dressed in work clothes. We had breakfast and afterward got in his truck.

We went to different homes in Hobbs, where I had to do manual labor all day. I mowed lawns, chopped weeds, raked leaves, picked up trash and washed windows. I had a lunch break around 1:00 P.M. and by evening I was starving. I finally got home around 5:30 that evening. I was tired and hungry. My step-dad told me that I could do manual labor for the rest of my life or I could go to school. That was a no brainer! I was glad to go to school the next day, and I don't remember missing any more days of school. Education was very important to my parents, and they did everything in their power to impress upon me the value of staying in school and getting a good education.

Chapter IV

Lessons Learned

The Bible tells us that we should train up a child in the way he should go and when he gets old he will not depart from his teachings. This formed the basis of my early childhood development. The entire community generally shared this view. Family after family became a part of the *village*, and child rearing became a major concern of the entire community. As a result, we had very few kids go astray, get arrested or even get in trouble with the police. We had pranksters, not gangsters. Our neighbors had almost as much influence on us as our parents did because our parents knew that our neighbors cared for us and wanted us to succeed. Child rearing was truly considered a community effort.

Once a few of my friends and I decided we were going to form a gang. We had talked about it for a couple of weeks and we decided to have a meeting at the Center. We had picked out a name for the gang; we called ourselves the "Blackhawks." The meeting had been underway for only a few minutes when in walks Jimmy Palmer, who was one of the black police officers in town and later became the Chief of Police for the City of Hobbs. To this day, I do not know how he found out about the meeting. (The night has a thousand eyes.) When he came in, he said, "I want you guys to know that there is only one Blackhawk in this town and that's me." The meeting was over and the Blackhawks disbanded on the spot. I still tremble when I say or hear the word "Blackhawk," or when I think of Jimmy Palmer. We got the message and it came through loud and clear. We had our wings clipped that day and the Blackhawks never got off the ground.

There were many messages that came to young people from older adults. Very few of them had any formal education beyond high school, and many did not even finish high school; yet, they had wisdom that formal education could not provide. Their wisdom was based on experience gained from the school of hard knocks. They did not have the B.A.s and the M.A.s or the Ph.D.s, but what they did have was common sense based on an instinct for survival, and this is what they passed on to the young. (Unfortunately, we came to a point in our history when the young stopped listening because they felt that this type of knowledge was obsolete.)

At an early age, I was taught that any job worth doing is worth doing right. This concept was drilled into me, and God only knows how many times I had to go back and do something over until it was done *right. No half steppin'. No short cuts. Take your time and get it right the first time and you won't have to worry about having to come back to do it again. Part of this concept was to do your very best. When you start something, finish it. Put your signature on it and you won't have to be ashamed.* I was taught that when you work for someone, regardless of what you were being paid, give more than required. That also says that in life we have to deposit more than we withdraw. By doing this, we leave something behind so that others are able to benefit from our efforts.

The values of my community were built on trust. I grew up in an era where a handshake was a binding agreement. If a person told you something and shook your hand, no paperwork was needed. No lawyers had to be present because a man's word was his bond. In later life, this concept has caused me a lot of hurt and embarrassment, especially in the political arena. I will elaborate more on this in a later chapter. The world I grew up in was based on truth. *Tell the truth, it's the easiest thing to remember.* One of the worse things that a person could be known as was a liar. Even if a lie would give you an escape or a way out, I was told that it was still best to stand on the truth. This value would be tested many times in my life, but I would rather be known as someone who made a mistake and admitted it, than someone who lied and the lie was uncovered later. When the lie is uncovered, the person moves from a suspected liar to a confirmed liar. I never wanted to be in either category.

Another value that was drilled into me is that something is either right *or* it's wrong. Something is either black or white. When black and white come together you have gray in between. When we look for the gray in between, that's when we get in trouble. If one believes that something is right, then you must stand on that regardless of what or who is on the other side. *No challenge, no change*. Taking a stand can have many ramifications. It can damage or destroy your reputation, and cause you to lose friends. You can be ostracized; have loss of pay, denial of promotions and other nasty things that the system can do. On the other hand, if you stand for what is right you will be known as a person of integrity and that's when God takes over.

Life was hard and by the standards of that day, we would have been classified as *poor*. However, I remember always having something to eat. We grew a lot of our own fruits and vegetables, and once a year my Mom would can the vegetables and store them for the winter. In the spring of each year a man by the name of Mr. Eli would come by with his mule and plow up the vacant lot next to our house. Then my step-dad would plant seeds for vegetables for the year. He planted corn, squash, black-eyed peas, green beans, assorted greens and other types of vegetables.

We grew enough food to get us through the winter. We lived on the edge of town and rabbits were plentiful. We ate fried rabbit, rabbit in gravy, rabbit sausage and rabbit patties. We had chickens in our backyard, so eggs were no problem. We also raised hogs, which we slaughtered in the fall of the year. So we were not destitute when it came to food. We could not afford to see a medical doctor, so when we got sick home remedies seemed to work just fine. Our people had to be resourceful if they were to survive.

Growing up, the majority of my social activities were centered on the church. I was expected, no, required to go to church every Sunday. As mentioned earlier, no work was to be done on Sunday. Mom cooked Sunday's meal on Saturday. Clothes were ironed on Saturday. Sunday was the Lord's Day, and I mean it was the Lord's Day. At 9:30 in the morning was Sunday School and 11:00 was morning worship service. We were out by 1:00 p.m. or 1:30. We would go home and eat and be back to church by 6:00 for BYPU (Baptist Young Peoples' Union). After that, we had night service at 7:00 in the evening. This was truly, the Lord's Day.

Strict discipline was adhered to in the church. No talking was allowed during church services. If I was caught talking, my mother would give me a cold stare over her glasses from the choir stand. I knew there was trouble around the bend, and I knew that issue would be dealt with when we got home. There also was no gum chewing. If you got caught chewing gum, an usher would come to you, grab your jaws on each side with one hand and force your mouth open. She would have a tissue in the other hand and would squeeze your jaws until the gum came out onto the tissue. This was done in front of the entire congregation and, of course, Mom was watching.

Along with lying, stealing was an unacceptable offense. Taking things that did not belong to you would be dealt with swiftly because there was no excuse for stealing. Stealing food because you were hungry was no excuse. If you did not work, you didn't deserve to eat. Someone once stole another man's toolbox, and I heard that not only did he lose his tools, but he also lost the opportunity to continue to make a living for himself and take care of his family.

I grew up believing that there is no such word as *can't*. Can't is can with an apostrophe t. Every problem has a solution and the only obstacles that I had in life were the ones that I was willing to accept. *The path to the top is full of obstacles, but there is a way over, around or through these obstacles. We need to trust that God will see us through.* This has always worked for me. If we place our destiny in the hands of God *no weapon formed against thee shall prosper*.

Thus, I looked at racism and racist behavior as being opposed to the will of God. God does not accept it; neither should we. I knew that this was not the way that God intended for things to be and His will shall be done. Racism will one day be a thing of the past. I may not see the end in my lifetime, but one thing I am convinced of is that one day *racism will end.*

I grew up developing a strong sense of justice and fairness. I later developed the attitude that racism must be confronted, no matter where it comes from and whenever it rears its ugly head. We cannot eliminate all of the racism at one time. We have to dismantle racism piece by piece and eliminate the tentacle of racism before it grows to a larger monster that will ultimately consume us all.

My belief is that you can't fail at something unless you try. Failure is not the end of the line, but a learning experience that can lead to success the next time around. Setbacks and adversity can only make us stronger; therefore I have never been reluctant to try new things, forge new ground or take on the system. I decided many years ago not to have any regrets about things I have done and to not make excuses. We make choices in life, and excuses open the back door so that we don't have to own up to our actions. There is something dishonest about making excuses. Excuses afford us the opportunity to procrastinate and to become stagnant. Something stagnant is something that is not growing or moving. Excuses also give people a hiding place. Thank God, I never used my race as an excuse not to try new things. I may be at a disadvantage because I am black, but that means I have to put my trust in God and work a little harder to close the gap .

A value I learned early in life was that we, as African Americans, had to work harder and get more education than the white man in order to move ahead. That seemed unfair, but in an unequal world, that statement was (and still is) a painful reality. We were told that we had to be twice as good to even be considered and that education was not only a way out, but also a way up. Norman Vincent Peale once said, "Whatever the mind can conceive and the heart can believe, you can achieve." This is one of the principles by which I live my life.

Chapter V

Fly Like an Eagle

During my younger days, especially around 1955-56, the desire most boys had was to be a Hobbs Eagle, to play on the Hobbs High basketball team, and to be coached by Ralph Tasker. Many of us wanted to be a part of the great tradition established by former players such as Bill Bridges, Ray Clay and Kim Nash. To be coached by Ralph Tasker placed a player in a special company of young men that only a select few would have the privilege to enjoy.

I remember one day in junior high school, Coach Tasker came to one of our basketball practices. You would have thought the President of the United States of America had just walked in. I knew then that I wanted to play on his team. My burning desire was to be a Hobbs Eagle.

I was determined to make the team; all I needed was the opportunity to show what I could do. Every available moment I had, I worked on my basketball skills. I would play with some of the older guys so that I could get better. No matter what, I *had* to become a Hobbs Eagle!

During my sophomore year in high school, I was selected for the "B" team. I was one step closer to my ultimate goal. I was fortunate to have Gene Ashmore as my "B" team coach. He was a good teacher, a good motivator and a good coach. I learned a lot under him. After my sophomore year, I went to the gym every day during the summer and shot 100 jump shots over a high bar from different points. I *had* to be a Hobbs Eagle! I wanted to play for Ralph Tasker.

At Hobbs High School, I played football, basketball and was a high jumper on the track team. During my junior year, I excelled on the football team. I looked forward to my senior year because I showed a great deal of promise as a football player and I was expected to have a good senior year. Racism has a way of rearing its ugly head in any situation, even on the football field. In 1959, the school hired a new football coach, Joe Mobra, from Oklahoma. When he came in, black football players began to drop off the team one by one. He had never worked with black football players before, and he felt that he could win with only white players. I really loved playing football and basketball, but I was probably a lot better at football. After my junior year, I was predicted to be All-State in football my senior year. I looked around one afternoon at football practice and there were only two black players left on the team.

I was determined to stick it out. I became oblivious to the yelling and screaming and the humiliation of being relegated to second string, losing my position to a 155-pound white sophomore. I put up with not being allowed to practice plays during practice sessions. I remember one scrimmage game against Portales. The kid who replaced me got hurt and Coach Mobra put me in the game. The quarterback called a play that required me to run straight-ahead five yards and cut across the middle of the field. The quarterback threw the ball behind me and by instinct I reached back and caught the ball with one hand. The result, after I avoided several tacklers, was a touchdown. When I returned to the sideline, Coach Mobra gave me a severe tongue-lashing because I caught the ball with one hand. He said that I was "showboating" or "showing off." The next day he called me into his office and continued his tongue-lashing. He said that as long as he was coach, no nigger was ever going to play on his team. I left his office, went to my locker, turned in my uniform and never looked back.

Coach Mobra made his choice and I made mine. My football career ended that day. A week later, the last black player quit the team. Hobbs High School had a lily white football team and a losing season. Joe Mobra was asked to leave the following year.

As a basketball player, I made the Varsity team my junior and senior years. On the road trips the black players had rooms together and so did the white players. Although we all got along well together, we seldom socialized with one another because we were not allowed to go where the white kids could go.

Once we took a road trip to Lawton and Duncan, Oklahoma. Reservations at the hotel were made in advance. When we arrived in Lawton and we all got out of the two station wagons, the bellman came out and informed us that the white players could stay at the hotel, but the black players could not. Coach Tasker turned red with anger. He came over and informed us that we could turn around and go back home or we could make other arrangements. Well, things were no different back in Hobbs. We told Coach Tasker that we came to play basketball and that we would get our revenge on the court and go home victorious. Arrangements were made for us to stay in private homes of black families in the town.

I recall that during one game in Portales, Coach Tasker had five black ball players on the floor at the same time. This was not done in the early '60s. I am convinced that Coach saw talent rather than color. We heard the name-calling and felt the displeasure from the Portales fans. Then all of a sudden their band started playing *Sweet Georgia Brown,* which was the theme song for the Harlem Globetrotters. When the game was over, someone threw a rock through a window while we were getting dressed. Thank God, no one was injured.

There were basketball players who had skills far superior to mine. There were those who could run faster, jump higher and shoot with greater accuracy. But my approach to the game was that there would never be a player, either on my team or the opposing team, who would outwork me. I would often ask Coach Tasker to let me guard the best player on the opposing team. I did not care how tall he was, and I was not impressed by his scoring average per game. I wanted to guard him because I was determined to work harder.

Playing for Coach Tasker taught me many lessons about life. One of the most valuable lessons we were taught was to have pride in yourself, your school and your team. Often he would call time out and in the huddle he would say, "you guys are not playing like Hobbs Eagles." I never heard him yell or scream at us. He was a quiet, gentle, soft-spoken man. But when he spoke, you knew he meant business. He was affectionately called "Tip" because he was "tip tops." It was an honor to play on a team for Ralph Tasker.

Coach Tasker ran the full-court press. Whether we were behind in points or ahead, he ran the press. I learned from him that life is a full-court press. We must keep the pressure on our opponents and ourselves in order to be successful. Whether you win or lose, you can still be successful if you do your best. When you do your very best, you are a winner, regardless of what someone else says. In my senior year as a Hobbs Eagle I went on to become All-State. I represented the South in the North/South All-Star game in August of 1960. Opportunity along with hard work will always pay off. I received a scholarship to attend college because of my hard work on the basketball court.

Race and racism always played a significant role in black/white relations in Hobbs. Everyone and everything had a *place*. When something or someone was found out of place, things started to *rattle* and the push was on to put things back in place or to find a way to minimize the rattle.

As black students at Hobbs High, we questioned why there had never been a black cheerleader at the school, and we said that the time had come to integrate the cheerleading squad. The president of the School Board, who was also the owner of the local radio station, was quoted as saying "over my dead body will a nigger be a cheerleader at Hobbs High." The cheerleaders were usually girls who came from the more prominent families in the community. They were usually selected, or I should say *pre-selected,* as sophomores. If a black girl was selected, one of the white girls would lose her slot. This was not going to happen in Hobbs during 1959-60.

As I look back, another incident occurred that shows how deeply racism was engrained into the cultural fabric of Hobbs. The White Establishment had a real dilemma during my senior year. The custom at Hobbs High was that the captain of the basketball team would escort the Homecoming Queen during half-time activities. Well, the captain of the team was Hollice Clay, who was black, and incidentally one of the best basketball and all-around athletes to attend Hobbs High School. The Homecoming Queen was white. *Big Problem.* This meant that a black male would appear with a white female holding his hand. NO WAY! This amused us black players because we wanted to see how they would get around this dilemma.

The administration and School Board members held several meetings. Finally, they came up with a solution that was acceptable to the white community, but an insult to the black community. They *selected* a black girl to be a member of the

Queen's Court, and the black captain of the team escorted her, while a white player escorted the white Queen. Had we protested this or made any noise about this arrangement, I believe we would have encountered grave consequences.

That experience was a painful reminder that there were two positions one could hold in Hobbs – superior and inferior. Both positions were based on race. When a person grows up with this concept drilled into him from birth and there is no one to tell him any different, although things are unacceptable, the notion is to believe that this is the way things are and there is nothing that he can do about it.

As young people, we used to discuss race problems among ourselves because we knew the boundaries and we often wondered what would happen if we stretched those boundaries. During the summer of 1960, five of my friends and I were riding around one Sunday afternoon. We decided to enter McClellans Department Store and order a hamburger at the lunch counter. Blacks were not served at the lunch counters at this time. It was against the *rules* for blacks and whites to eat together. This would make them equals. We sat down and the waitress came over and we told her that we wanted to order a hamburger.

She responded, "I'm sorry, we don't serve colored people here."

A friend of mine said, "We didn't order colored people, we ordered a hamburger."

We all had to laugh at that one. We asked, "Why?" She said that it was store policy and if she had anything to say about it, she would serve us. We asked to speak to the manager. He emphasized that it was not "his" policy, but policy established by the home office.

I asked him, "Why is it that we can come into your store and buy several dollars worth of clothing or other items, but we can't buy a fifty cent-hamburger?"

He said, "We can fix burgers to go, but you can't eat them here."

A tiny flame started to burn inside me after that. I came to the conclusion that this is not right. The newspaper reported the next day that "the sit-in movement has come to Hobbs, New Mexico." The paper went on to report that the people who tried to integrate the lunch counter did not look as though they were from Hobbs. Some of the black *leaders* in the community gave us a stern talking to about our *place*.

During April of my senior year, a light bulb went off in my head and I came to the realization that in a few short weeks I would be graduating from high school. I did not have a clue as to what I was going to do beyond graduation. During my generation, if you were male, when you turned 18 and graduated from high school, you left home. It was an unwritten cultural rule that you were to no longer be a burden to your parents. It was time to grow up and be a man and assume total responsibility for your own life.

I decided to talk to one of the advisors at Hobbs High to explore some options. His advice to me was to join the Army. At that time, I didn't consider that to be a viable option. At 18 years of age, a two-year commitment to anything seemed like a lifetime. Plus, I was afraid that they would send me off to some far away place. I had never been outside of Hobbs except on athletic trips or to visit my aunt and uncle who lived 100 miles away. Joining the Army was the only option presented to me. I asked him about college and his words still ring in my ears today, "College is not for everyone. You would probably be wasting your time and money if you went to college." I had friends who had signed up for the service, some to the Air Force and some the Navy, so I came to the conclusion that the Army was the only option open to me. I did not want to stay in Hobbs. I could not go to college. I knew I had to do something, so I embraced (not too tightly) the idea of going to the Army. However, I put that decision off to the point of procrastination.

During the month of May, I received a letter in the mail inviting me to participate in the North/South All-Star basketball game. My intentions were to get in shape and forget about the Army until after August. I would participate in the All-Star game and when the game was over, then I would join the Army.

I played a lot of basketball during the summer; then I went to Albuquerque and checked into the dormitory at the University of New Mexico. Eating meals at Polly's Restaurant was one of the highlights of that All-Star experience. Did we pig out! I loved Polly's; the food was great! Also, being associated with a great bunch of young men was fantastic. I cannot remember the name of the coach for the South team, but he was from Eunice, New Mexico. He was a good coach and a fair individual. I totally enjoyed the experience.

After the game, I was in the locker room removing my tennis shoes and a gentleman came up to me and introduced himself. His name was Joe Kleoppel, and he had recently been hired to be the basketball coach at St. Joseph College on the Rio Grande. I remember his words, "How would you like to come and play basketball at the College of St. Joseph?" My response, "I don't think so, I would be wasting my time and your money." He was stunned! He wanted to know why I would make a statement like that. I told him what the advisor had told me at Hobbs High.

Coach Kleoppel told me that I should make my own decision and at least give it a try. I learned later that one of the biggest failures we can experience is not trying. If you do not try, you fail anyway. If you try and fail, you learn from the experience. So we had another conversation and I decided to give college and college basketball a try. Besides, I really did not want to go to the Army. So, by default, I went to college. Coach Kleoppel took a personal interest in me and helped me through some very difficult challenges during my first year in college.

Chapter VI

What Am I Doing Here?

In 1960, after my arrival in Albuquerque to attend St. Joseph's College, I asked myself, *What am I doing here*? My dad brought me to Albuquerque on a Friday and I stayed with one of his friends until school started. I saw his friend when we arrived, and I didn't see him anymore during the weekend I stayed there. I did not know where I was and I did not know a soul in the city. Since registration was not until Monday morning. I asked myself over and over, *What am I doing here*? To make things worse, I had no car, the TV was fuzzy, and the man whose home I occupied, being a bachelor, had no food. There was a grocery store around the corner. My financial resources were limited, so I had to stretch things out to last over the weekend.

I was homesick before school even started. I thought about taking the bus back home, but I thought about the look in my mother's eyes when I told her that I was going to college and I knew the pride she had felt when I left home. I *could not go back.* I had to make it until Monday. Things would be different then. So I watched that fuzzy TV and I ate baloney sandwiches until Monday. Monday would be the turning point in my life, but I kept asking myself, *What am I doing here?* When I thought about Mom, the question was answered. The commitment had been made. I could not look in my mother's eyes and tell her that I failed because I didn't try.

That Monday morning, the athletic director Rudy Cordova picked me up and drove me out to the college. We took a winding road to the middle of nowhere. *What am I doing here?* came to mind again. The college sat upon a bluff on the northwest mesa. There were no streets, no houses and no stores. What had I gotten myself into? When I arrived on campus, I saw a familiar face, Isidro Garcia! We had played on the same All-Star team. I don't know how Estancia qualified as a southern city, but I am glad that he was on my team. Isidro was probably the best basketball player the College of St. Joseph ever produced. I felt better; I had found someone I knew. The rest came easy and I formed some friendships that have lasted over 40 years.

My years at the College of St. Joseph were very enjoyable, in spite of the fact that shortly after school began a student called me a nigger. My new friends, who were non-black, took care of the situation. They took him aside and talked to him. I don't know what they said, but that student later came to me and apologized.

When I entered college, there were only five black students on campus. This was a real culture shock for me. I had to learn how to function in a multi-cultural, multi-ethnic and multi-religious environment. The College of St. Joseph on the Rio Grande was a cultural learning laboratory. I learned more about Hispanic and Native Americans than I had ever imagined. New worlds were unfolding almost on a daily basis. Foods that I had never known existed were now at my fingertips.

I recall the first time that I went to a Mexican restaurant. It was called "Fitos," located on Fourth and Bridge and I ordered a bowl of chili. They brought this bowl of "green stuff." I figured that the waitress misunderstood, so I told her again that I wanted chili, *real* chili. She informed me that there were only two types of chili in the world, red or green. This did not look like the chili I ate in Hobbs. But, I decided to try the "green stuff" and I have been addicted ever since.

My friends and classmates on campus were great. I had very few racial problems on campus. Off campus in Albuquerque was a different story. I remember talking to some friends on a corner in Albuquerque and a police officer came by and told us to "break it up." Four blacks congregating on a corner in downtown Albuquerque was unacceptable. During my junior year, an officer stopped me and gave me a ticket for "changing lanes without a signal." This was one of many incidents where I felt uneasy with a police officer. I did not put my signal light on because there were no cars either in front or behind me. He told me to start my car and press the gas pedal. He gave me another ticket for having a loud muffler. I kept my mouth shut and accepted the ticket.

I took the ticket to court and Judge Robbins heard the case. He said, "There is something about this that does not smell right. Case dismissed." The police officer later went on to become an assistant United States Attorney.

One of the low points of my college days at St. Joseph was being kicked off the basketball team. Why it happened will never be answered because Rudy Cordova, the man who did this, is no longer alive. He caught a group of basketball players, along with some baseball players, drinking beer. Another basketball player and I were downtown at the public library researching a term paper. The two of us, as well as those who were drinking the beer, were kicked off the teams. I never understood his actions, because he kept other players on the team. I tried to talk to him on a couple of occasions, but he refused to discuss the matter. I deserved an answer, but it went to the grave with him.

Many years ago, I forgave Rudy Cordova in my heart, and now I am at peace with that unfortunate and unfair situation. I am of the opinion that there comes a time in life when one has to let things go and move on. Holding on to the past can only hold you down. There are too many challenges ahead of us to get bogged down by those issues that have already passed.

I had to make a decision that would determine the course of my life from that point on *do I transfer to another college or do I stay at St. Joseph's?* I had to evaluate the other question also, *why am I here?* I concluded that I was at the College of St. Joseph to get an education. Basketball was a vehicle I had used, but basketball was secondary. I could get an education without basketball. Whatever it took, I was determined to get my degree and my degree would read College of St. Joseph. Once I made that decision, God took over from there.

After the incident with the basketball team, I decided to get serious about school and the reality that my basketball playing days might be over. I somehow knew that the opportunity to play again would eventually come around. I also knew that whether I played again would be *my* decision. God works that way sometimes. I was asked to come back and play the following season. By that time I had put things in perspective – education was the most important thing in my life. I remember Mom's words, "Get an education! That's something the white man can never take from you." I realized that no matter how good you are, basketball can be taken away, but education is something that will always remain.

I was always interested in history and I decided to make that my major, along with physical education (I wanted to become a coach). I had a history professor who did not like athletes or athletics. As far as he was concerned, neither belonged on a college campus. He made it very difficult for me in class. He singled me out during the semester, and on several occasions I felt ridiculed. I made the decision to hang in there because if I was going to major in history there was no way around him. Besides, I had two other history professors, Dr. McGrath and Warren Lee, who stimulated me and encouraged me in my pursuit. The majority of the professors at the college were fair and encouraging.

When I rejoined the basketball team, a new coach had been hired. He had a practice of filling out the class schedules for the athletes. We had to take the classes he wanted us to take so that we could remain eligible to play on the team.

During the first semester of my junior year, I got my class schedule, went to the bookstore and got my books. The class schedule, signed by the coach, is what triggered my registration. One day I looked at the college catalog and discovered that the courses I was taking were not leading toward graduation. The next semester I "borrowed" some of the class schedule forms from the coach's desk. I filled out the forms myself using the college catalog as a guide, signed his name, got my books and went to class. Essentially, I took the more challenging classes that would lead to graduation rather than the classes the coach wanted me to take to ensure that I would remain eligible to play on the team. He never knew what I had done. I was determined to graduate.

After my junior year I was told that I was six hours short for graduating on time. I told my coach that I needed to go to summer school to pick up those six hours. He told me that he did not have money in his budget to cover the cost. I told him that it was important for me to graduate on time. He said that if I waited until the following summer he would cover the cost. I reminded him that the following summer I would have no eligibility left. I needed to go *this* summer or I would not play basketball my senior year. I took six hours of course credit during that summer. My relationship with the coach changed, but I got my degree on schedule. *No challenge, no change*!

I mentioned before that many friendships were formed during my college days. In a way, a few of us became *brothers*. We found ourselves in a common situation because none of us had money, but we shared what we had. We were all struggling to get a degree and we hung out together. Color did not matter; class was not an issue, and we really did like one another and we got along. We called ourselves the "Hobos." A person had to be special to be in this fraternity. One had to be able to drink a few beers, party on the weekends or whenever the occasion arose, and one's behavior had to be a little bizarre. But most of all one had to study and stay in school. We are still in contact after all these years. We shared a common experience and a common bond. Even today, the bond is still strong.

During my senior year, our team was selected to play in the NAIA Tournament in Kansas City, Missouri. At the banquet that was sponsored for the players I had the opportunity to meet then Vice President Richard Nixon and shake his hand.

I did my student teaching at John Adams Middle School in Albuquerque and I graduated in May of 1964 with a Bachelor of Science Degree in Education. I had reached my goal! The time had come to face the future.

My first teaching job in the Albuquerque Public School System (APS) was at Sandoval Elementary School in Corrales, New Mexico. The school was under the authority of APS at the time. I taught physical education and the kids called me "Coach." Little did I know when I was hired that I would meet a man who would change my life. His name was Dever Langholf and he was the principal of Sandoval Elementary School. Because of him, I wanted to become a principal, but I knew that at that time, because of my race, it was not possible with APS. I was with Dever for two years.

Probably the most defining moment in our relationship was in April of 1968 when Dr. Martin Luther King, Jr. was assassinated. I drove to school with tears in my eyes; I felt hurt, angry, confused and helpless. When I arrived at school, I felt that I really did not want to be there – but I did not know where I wanted to be. Again, I asked myself the question, *What am I doing here*? I should have learned from the assassination that the front line is a dangerous place for a black man to be. It is not safe to confront racism in America because when you do, there is a wide range of repercussions that you will face.

I recall sitting alone in the teachers' lounge when Dever walked in. He said, "This is a sad day for all of us. Come and go with me." We walked out to the front of the school. I wondered, *What is this about? Where is he taking me*? I really just wanted to be alone. We walked together to the flagpole and he said, "Let's lower the flag to half mast." And we did. I felt better. A special moment in history, shared by two men of diverse backgrounds made a statement that the world needed to hear - there are people of compassion who care about the welfare of others. Because of what he did, there will forever be a bond between us. Too bad we could not make that statement to the world. When people come together as human beings, they can change the world.

Dever saw something in me that I did not see in myself, so, he recommended me for the Leadership Development Program funded by the Ford Foundation. This was a year-long program and was designed to provide a fellowship for individuals who demonstrated leadership potential in the field of education. When chosen, each fellow could design a program that would enhance his knowledge of leadership principles in education. Fellows were to make their own connections and observe programs that were making a difference in the field of education.

My first involvement as a Ford Foundation Fellow was with a minority recruitment program that reached out to high school seniors and encouraged them to attend college. The targeted students came from rural communities in New Mexico. I went to many of the high schools in northern New Mexico and visited homes to talk with the kids. I ate a lot of chili and beans in these homes. It was a great experience because I was able to help some kids who never knew that college was possible for them.

After my involvement with this program ended and I had completed work on my Masters Degree, my next stop was an internship at Duke University, with the Education Improvement Program. This was a university-sponsored program designed to enhance the learning opportunities for minority children in the community. I was impressed with this program because I observed minority third graders learning three languages at the same time. They were speaking English, French and Spanish. Also impressive was their enthusiasm and eagerness to learn.

I was able to become involved with the black community in Durham, North Carolina, by being a part of an organization that was committed to community change through activism and implementing programs for community improvement. I had never had this kind of exposure to black leadership before who confronted the system and spoke up for their people. Neither had I ever witnessed the kind of resistance that these courageous black leaders were up against, namely the Ku Klux Klan.

I also took a tour of the North Carolina Mutual Insurance Company: a black-owned insurance enterprise. My eyes were opened to a whole new world. Black people *owned* this multi-million dollar company. The majority of the employees were black and the building, which was expansive, was very impressive. I had the opportunity to meet some of the executives and the other employees. I left that building with a feeling of pride. I came to the conclusion that the way to freedom and security is to build your own and hire your own. You can provide job opportunities in your own community for your own people. This was quite a revelation.

I arrived in Durham at the tail end of an economic boycott. The black community had sponsored a black Christmas parade to counteract the annual Christmas parade sponsored by the white community. The intent was to keep African Americans from shopping in downtown stores. I was told that the overall boycott was quite effective. It brought blacks and whites to the table to work out improvement in the black community.

During my involvement in Durham, I became keenly aware of race and race relations. I knew then that whenever racism reared its ugly head it had to be dealt with and the best way to deal with racism was to confront it head on. If racism was not challenged, there could be no change. I also realized that once you confronted racism and spoke out, you had to be prepared to pay a price. Racism or a racist does not sneak away quietly into the night. If it does, it will come back in another form or return with help. Power might be on the side of those who inflict injustice on others, but God is on the side of the just. I believe strongly that the "meek shall inherit the earth."

After leaving Durham and Duke University, I went to New York where I attended Teachers' College at Columbia University. I took nine hours of class work and volunteered at a Street Academy, an alternative school for kids who were *pushed* out of high school.

At Columbia, one of the classes I enrolled in was Afro-American History. This course was offered as an undergraduate level course. I wanted to broaden my knowledge of black history, so since I was not working on a graduate degree, I felt that this would be an informational course to provide knowledge I could use later. The class was quite large and had generated a lot of interest because the black students had pushed for it. The majority of the students were black.

The first day of class, the instructor walked in and stepped up to the podium. A sudden quietness came over the class. He was a white man! The students waited a few minutes, as if they wanted to see if he was going to make an announcement or teach the class. He said, "My name is Eric Foner, Jr. I am your teacher for this class." One of the more vocal students called for a boycott of the class and he urged all black students to walk out. Every black student in the room walked out. The student who called for the boycott was a young man I came to know later, Ralph Metcalf, Jr., the son of the late Congressman from Chicago. Eric Foner, Jr. was one of the leading authorities on black history in the United States, and the students walked out on this opportunity.

I talked to Professor Foner and proposed that we establish a dialogue with the black student leadership. We were able to reach a compromise. Since I was not an undergraduate student and I had just obtained a Masters Degree, I offered to grade the papers of any black student who felt more comfortable with me. The students agreed and I was given the title of "Graduate Assistant." I graded several papers, but more importantly I was able to take this class and work with this outstanding professor.

At that time, New York City was full of cultural and political activity. I saw students protest and take over the administration building at Columbia. This was quite a shock – these were white students! *What were* ***they*** *ticked off about*? I wondered to myself.

Morningside Park separates Columbia University from Harlem. I used to walk to 125th Street, over to Lennox Avenue and hear street corner speakers talk about some of the issues of the day. I would spend hours in the Schoemberg Library in Harlem. Bookstores were bursting at the seams with black literature. Speakers and literature and activity were all around. I wanted to take it all in. My life began to take on a new direction. This experience was making me more aware of my surroundings. New York was a magnificent city!

The volunteer work I did at the Street Academy was probably one of the most eye-opening experiences I ever had. I began to understand kids who had problems in the traditional school setting and how to help them reach their potential. The assignment I had at the Academy was to teach reading. To reach these kids, I had to use some non-traditional methods. These methods could not be employed in a traditional school. I told the students that they could bring in any book or magazine they so desired for their reading assignments. I know that a few tried to shock me with the materials they brought in. My strategy was to move them from *Playboy* to Shakespeare, from *Penthouse* to Poe. The strategy worked. It was gradual, but I got those kids excited about reading.

I probably learned more from these kids than they could ever have gotten from me. Although they were *push outs*, I found most of them to be very creative and very inquisitive. They were hungry for knowledge, but it had to be fed to them in a manner that was acceptable to them. Once teachers can go to that place where a child is dwelling, and stay there for a while, we can lead him to where we would like for him to go. I went to that dwelling place and I stayed there for a while and I used that creativity to open new worlds for my students.

One student – I will call him Jose, a Puerto Rican teen – had a talent for writing poetry. I had him read books and articles, and write poems and short stories about what he read. We got together a collection of his poems, typed them, placed a cover on them and made a booklet. He was so proud! So was I! Jose had been on and off drugs, but he was so excited about his writing that he told me he was clean and would never do drugs again. He worked hard and took every opportunity presented to improve his writing skills. I heard about a summer poetry writing program at Yale University that was designed for young people like Jose. I encouraged him to apply. We waited and waited for a response. One day, Jose came in with his letter. He handed me the letter and went to the bathroom. When he came out, his eyes and nose were red and watery. Jose left the Street Academy that day and he never returned. After all these years, I often wonder what happened to Jose.

Across the street from the Street Academy were a funeral home and a candy store. Big, late model cars drove up to the funeral home every day. After a couple of months, I asked the director of the Street Academy, "How do those guys stay in business? I have never seen them have a funeral at that place." He told me that the funeral home was a "front." Drugs were being sold out of the candy store and the guys next door were watching their business. There were an awful lot of young people going in and out of that "candy store." I remember one of my students asking me one day, *Mr. Becknell, why is it that a fifth grade student can find a pusher but the police can't*? That question still burns in my mind to this day.

I wrapped up the New York portion of my fellowship in May of 1969. The next stop was Washington, D.C. I served as an intern with the House Education and Labor Committee. Adam Clayton Powell was the chairman. I never got the opportunity to meet him personally, but he was responsible for pushing through legislation regarding student loans and grants that allowed many minority and low income students to attend college.

Next, the fellowship took me to Los Angeles, California, where I interned with State Senator Mervyn Dymally, who sponsored the Urban Affairs Institute. He was one of the first to openly speak about the deplorable conditions in state prisons in California. Dymally was one of the most insightful and impressive men I have ever met. He later went on to become a U.S. Congressman.

I had the opportunity to spend some time with him in Sacramento. I followed him around, sat in on meetings, and had lunch with him and some of his colleagues. The rest of the fellowship I spent in a summer program for minority kids in the Los Angeles area.

I returned to Albuquerque in August of 1969. I knew that Albuquerque Public Schools (APS) was going to provide me with the opportunity to put all of this newly acquired knowledge to good use in the system. I had requested to be assigned to teach history at Albuquerque High School. APS denied my request and reassigned me to my old job teaching PE at Sandoval Elementary. I refused to go and stayed home. Ted Martinez, who was President of the Board of Education, opened the door for me to teach at Albuquerque High School. He called the principal and told him that time and opportunity had presented itself and that this course needed to be taught. He allocated another position to the school. I taught African American History at Albuquerque High for one year.

My teaching experience at Albuquerque High School was a big eye opener. I realized that there was a tremendous need for black history to be taught, not only at this school, but in every school in the district. There was also a great need to teach the history of Hispanics as well. The ratio of Hispanic to black students almost dictated that Hispanics receive consideration. The nature of the topic and the turbulent times this country was going through caused me to be viewed with suspicion by the principal and a large number of the Anglo faculty. With the exception of a handful of faculty members, I spent that year (1969-70) at Albbquerque High in virtual isolation. I was the campus *radical*, the person to avoid.

One of the people I admired at Albuquerque High was Jim Hulsman. He had recently been hired as the boys' basketball coach and one day he asked if we could go across the street and have a cup of coffee. Coach Hulsman asked my opinion about how to handle his concern regarding the long Afro hairstyles, sideburns and facial hairs that was proudly worn by the African American players. The coach wore his hair closely cut. He did not like long hair, but he wanted more insight into the matter. I advised him to explain to the players how he felt and that he was not trying to take anything from them, but trying to bring about team unity. I advised him to meet the players halfway. That approach worked out well.

During another instance, Coach Hulsman invited me to the drug store for a cup of coffee. He asked me how to beat the full-court press used by the Hobbs basketball team. I diagramed the strategy on a napkin. He went on to decimate the Hobbs press and win a State Championship. I never told Coach Tasker, the Hobbs basketball coach, what I had done. Coach Hulsman, Jess Miranda and Moises Venegas were the only faculty members who extended friendship to me during my year at Albuquerque High School.

I recall some of the students in a World History class asking me to come to their class and lecture on African History. I told them that I could only come with an invitation from their teacher. They asked their teacher and her reply was, "There is nothing to talk about; Africa has contributed nothing to world civilization." She had been teaching World History for 32 years!

The African American students at Albuquerque High in 1969-70 were a special group of young people. I am proud to have been a part of their lives. At their 20-year reunion, several of these young men and women attended church service that Sunday. I had recently been called to pastor Mt. Olive Baptist Church. I stepped out to deliver my sermon and I was surprised to see them. A spokesperson for the group told the congregation that the prior evening they had been discussing their high school experiences. They got around to the topic of which teacher had the greatest influence on their lives. They decided that I was the one and they wanted to come to church and say "thank you." I had to compose myself before I could speak. To have your students come back and say "thank you" is the highest tribute that a teacher can receive. Besides being the pastor of a local church, teaching is the best job I have ever had.

Chapter VII

Changing the World: The Making of an Activist

During the early '70s, I saw so much wrong with the world. Due to my youthful idealism, I was going to change everything, starting with Albuquerque, then the State of New Mexico, after that the United States of America and why not the world? I wanted everyone, especially my people, to get a fair shake. Injustice, in my mind, must be challenged and racism must be eliminated. I set out on a mission to make things better. I met a man who published an article about my views in the *Albuquerque News*. Arlen Asher wrote the article, but was encouraged by the editor, Fred McCaffrey. A friendship developed between McCaffrey and me that endured for many years until his death.

I began to speak out on many issues facing the African American community. I began to mobilize community people to organize and challenge the system for better treatment. I formed a friendship and bond with a community activist, John Goldsmith, a VISTA volunteer. It was under John's leadership that many improvements were made in the Albuquerque community. John had an intimidating presence. He was around six feet two inches, 250 pounds, he wore a large Afro and dark glasses. Underneath that exterior was one of the most considerate human beings I had ever met. He had a keen insight into political issues and an uncanny sense of strategy as to how to confront the system. His impact on the community will be felt for many years to come. He has not received the recognition due him for his efforts. Fred Ward later joined him and me and we set out to change Albuquerque for the better. These were men who were not afraid to challenge the system because they knew that if there was no challenge, the condition of African Americans would not improve. *No challenge, no change.*

Our major concern was addressing police relations in the black community. Numerous complaints were being received regarding black citizens who had had run-ins with the police. Racial profiling is nothing new! It has been going on for a long, long time. We formed an organization and named it the Black Coalition. We asked a number of black organizations to come together to stand against unfair treatment of black citizens by the police. I recall one of our Coalition meetings when we were discussing this issue and I had left something in my car. I went out to the parking lot and discovered a police officer taking down license plate numbers of the Coalition meeting participants.

Another incident occurred one day when John Goldsmith and I were on the way to Fred Ward's home and we were followed by two police officers. John was driving and he decided to pull over. When he did, the police officers drove past us. John then pulled out and followed behind them. We were stopped by these two officers and were given a ticket for following too close. We went to court and Judge Robbins dismissed the case. Several officers showed up in court that day, and they stormed out of the courtroom in disgust. Judge Robbins was not a popular man with the police that day.

I had dealings with every City of Albuquerque police chief from Chief Shaver to Chief Sam Baca. Chief Baca was a good man and a good chief. However, Bob Stover was probably the best to work with in terms of a good community working relationship. We did not trust him at first because he was previously the head of Internal Affairs for the Albuquerque Police Department. We felt that anyone in that position was there to protect the police and cover up any wrongdoing. So there was a natural distrust built in. When we had meetings with the Chief and Bob Stover was present, he very seldom said anything. We did not know where he was coming from. But when it was announced that he was going to be the new Chief of Police, he called Fred Ward and asked if he could meet with him and me. We met at Fred Ward's home where Bob Stover outlined some of his goals. He opened the door for a working relationship and at that meeting, mutual respect was gained and a friendship established. One of the first appointments made by Chief Stover was Don Thompson, an African American, to the position of Deputy Chief of Police.

During the turbulent days after Chief Stover, I discovered that if the world was to be changed, one had to first get past the police. They were the guardians of the status quo. They were the frontline of defense, consequently, the relationship between the black community and the police became more adversarial. It became clear that we had conflicting interests. Any challenge to the status quo brought out the police.

Police briefings were held on Monday mornings about the previous weeks activities of Black Coalition members. Sheets were passed out which contained a list of Black Coalition members' license numbers and where we *hung out*. We challenged this practice and I believe it was Chief Donald Byrd that put an end to it (so we were told).

Perhaps the most intense period of police/community conflict came immediately after the incident when State police officer Rosenbloom was murdered on Interstate 40. Three black men from the West Coast were accused of this murder. They had red, black and green flag symbols on their car and were identified as being members of the Republic of New Africa. Their aim was to obtain several Southern states as land to be occupied exclusively by blacks. These three men managed to elude police and hide out in Albuquerque for about three days. During that time, it was not safe for any black male to be on the streets of Albuquerque day or night. Horror stories were reported about some citizens having shotguns pulled on them and some having to lie on the ground, face down. It appeared that the entire black community was under suspicion and under siege.

The men who had committed this crime managed to call a wrecker service, hijacked the wrecker, and had the driver take them to the airport. They drove to a TWA airliner that was preparing to take-off. They boarded and hijacked the plane and went to Cuba. News reports indicated that one of them has since drowned while in Cuba, and I assume the other two are still there. The backlash felt by the black community was quite scary. It appeared that the entire black community of New Mexico was being held accountable for the actions of three men that we didn't even know.

During the summer of 1970, I took over a newly created position, Director of African American Studies, at the University of New Mexico (UNM). The students at UNM had pushed for the position and had written a convincing document called "To Break the Chains," which spelled out the need for the position and the program. I worked at UNM during some very turbulent and volatile times. Student activism, black and white, would be seen on most college campuses throughout the United States, and the University of New Mexico was no exception.

I acted as an advocate for African American students, but I also tried to be a positive role model. I knew that being on a campus where the majority of the faculty was white, they needed to see someone who looked like them. My concern for these students was that they would not let their activism interfere with their education. I helped them establish priorities and stick to them. Of course, when issues were challenged by students at UNM, I was accused of "putting them up to it."

A case in point revolves around the athletic boycott in 1973. The athletes came to Harold Bailey and me and said that they were fed up with how they were being treated and were going to refuse to play. We advised them that there was a lot on the line – they could lose scholarships, and there also would be repercussions from teachers and the community. They were quite adamant about going through with the boycott. We asked them if we could act as intermediaries and negotiate on their behalf. We had assessed the risks of doing this and we concluded that it was worth the risk. We would surely be seen as the "bad" guys, but we wanted to protect those student athletes and try to keep things from getting too far out of hand. The University started to play hard ball and the students started to dig in and we were caught in the middle. We were all on a roller coaster ride.

I learned a lot from that experience. Black athletes are used like Kleenex. When they are used up, they are tossed. After graduation, boosters usually hire white athletes into pretty substantial jobs. They go into real estate, insurance and property management, to name a few. Black athletes are usually forgotten once their playing days are over.

Black students on a university campus live in an alien world. The food in the cafeteria is different. The campus environment is different. There were many black students operating on the edge, in terms of financial support. I encountered some black students who were on the verge of withdrawing from school because they could not purchase soap, toothpaste and deodorant. They became "my kids," and I had to find a way to keep them in school. Black students were recruited and encouraged to attend UNM, but received very little financial or emotional support. I often approached the Director of Financial Aid, Jack Sheehan, and explained the situation to him. Jack Sheehan was a very special man and had a lot of compassion for students. If a student needed help, Jack Sheehan found a way. He kept a lot of students in school and changed their lives forever.

Until 1973 there had only been one African American, Bob Jones, in the Law School at UNM. He graduated in 1968. I was quite concerned about this statistic, and I approached the Dean of the Law School at that time, Fred Hart. I entered his office ready to do battle. I wanted to know why only one black person had attended UNM's School of Law. He showed a sensitivity that was rare at that time. He said, "Charles, we don't have a problem. We are after the same thing. We can either complain or we can so something about it." He had the same concerns but no applicants. He suggested that we work together to get black applicants. Fred Hart paved the way for many black students, and due to his compassion and understanding, two former black students are judges who sit proudly on the bench today. I learned a very valuable lesson from this experience. There is a time for confrontation, but cooperation and collaboration can get the job done effectively as well.

I also realized that in the majority of situations when you challenge the system, the system will make you pay. When you get out of place, the system will put you back in your "place." The punishment goes on because you are placed in a "box" that is hard to get out of. People, in general, do not see you as you are but how they remember you once were.

During my activism days, I received threatening phone calls, a sheet of paper with crosshairs mailed to my home, job denials for which I was qualified, and numerous investigations. I am probably the most investigated African American in New Mexico. I have been investigated by the FBI, APD (Albuquerque Police Department), State police, UNM Campus police, and only God knows who else. UNM maintained files on me in three different locations twenty years after I no longer worked there. These files were supposed to be purged, but I suspect that they are still around. This probably accounts for the fact that I have applied for twenty-two jobs at UNM over the years and received only two interviews. I stopped applying when a reliable source told me that a high ranking official said, *they are never going to hire you at UNM.* Yes, there is a price to pay for activism and the system will make you pay, despite your qualifications.

While at UNM, I continued to work on and eventually received my Ph.D. in American Studies in 1975. Again, I remembered what my mother told me, "education is something the white man can never take from you." It was not "given," it was earned. Thanks Mom!

My first encounter with the brutality of the political system was in 1974 when Governor Bruce King appointed me to the State Bicentennial Commission. At the time I was working at UNM as the Director of the African American Studies Program. My role was to bring a black perspective to the Commission and to provide input regarding the contributions of blacks in the State of New Mexico.

We, on the Commission, were provided with our first dilemma when a few began to refer to New Mexico as a tri-cultural state. I objected to this reference and I immediately became an outcast. Tri-cultural meant Anglo, Hispanic and Native American. The African American culture was being overlooked. The quandary for many on the Commission was how do you recognize a culture that you know nothing about? The history books did not include this culture, so what do we do?

The Commission had asked for designs for a bicentennial coin. The selection had been made and the tri-cultural theme was projected on the coin. I objected to the omission of the African American presence and I pushed for recognition. You can push the system, but when the system finds itself in a corner, it will push back. I was told that the decision had been made and there were no other options. I asked, "What is going to be on the other side of the coin?" The room became silent. I said that we did have an option. They had no design for the other side of the coin. So, I was charged with proposing to the Commission a design for the other side.

After some research I discovered that Estevanico was a Moorish explorer who had led a Spanish expedition into Arizona and New Mexico. Why not depict an image of Estevanico on the other side of the coin? I made this proposal to the Commission and it was accepted. I thought, "This is justice. We got locked out on one side, now we have the whole other side to ourselves." Well, racism began to rear its ugly head. Benny Atencio, a Native American, fired the first shot. His argument was that Estevanico brutalized Native American people and took advantage of Indian women. My rebuttal was that the Spaniards did far worse and if we recognized people by their character rather than their contributions, we would probably have to tear down Mount Rushmore. Next came an attack from Joe Mullens, a fellow Commissioner, who objected because Estevanico was a Moor. I don't know what that was all about. Governor King received letters from The Daughters of the American Revolution and only God knows who else.

I learned that Governor Bruce King was a political animal who would respond to political pressure. The issue was too hot, politically, for him and he had to find a solution. He appointed a committee, headed by Senator Tibo Chavez. He also appointed Don Perkins to the committee, an African American and former Dallas Cowboy football player. The big guns were brought out and I could see the steamroller coming in my direction. Senator Chavez opened the coffin, placed me in it, and Don Perkins put the nails in. Don led the charge and it was essentially black on black. A motion was made by Don Perkins and seconded by Tibo Chavez that Estevanico be removed from the coin.

I have been in many battles and I have lost a few, but this one really hurt because of the way the battle was lost. I left the meeting dejected, but I left with the full knowledge that I had done my best for my community. If nothing else came out of this struggle, the tri-cultural concept was brought to the forefront, and the community in general became aware that the black presence in New Mexico should not be ignored. The black struggle in New Mexico has always been a struggle for recognition and inclusion. This struggle still goes on today. I made a conscious decision at this point that whatever I had to do – whatever sacrifice I had to make to bring dignity and respect to my people – I would do it.

At that meeting, I rapidly came to the conclusion that before the meeting took place, a decision had been made, a deal had been cut and I would be "blown out of the water." The system pushed back and the system won. The battle had been lost, but the war for recognition and dignity for my people would go on. We all live to fight another day. I was defeated but not destroyed. I found out later that if you push harder and harder, the system would destroy you.

It was during this time that I realized that to fight this fight against racism, I needed more than courage – I needed more than intelligence – I needed my Savior, Jesus Christ back in my life. I had drifted away from my religious faith and I realized that there was a big void in my life. I was led to Mt. Olive Baptist Church, where the pastor was Reverend W. C. Trotter. He showed me how much I needed Christ in my life because He could help me through these struggles, if I relied upon Him.

I began to serve in the church as a Sunday School teacher and later as a deacon. This re-entry into my spirituality helped me get through a failing marriage and other personal crises that I was facing. Now I had a renewed strength and renewed faith. I could now go back out there and slay that dragon called racism. I recall quoting from Philippians 4:13, "I can do all things through Christ who strengthens me." I still cling to that scripture today.

I began to realize that the tactic of confrontation was no longer effective. Accordingly, the realization came to me that the struggle needed to shift to working from the inside. From 1973 until 1982, I, along with Fred Ward, co-chaired the New Mexico Black Leadership Conference. We wanted to see a greater involvement of African Americans on state and city boards and commissions. We also wanted to see more African Americans in politically appointed positions in local and state government. The concept was that if African Americans were in decision-making positions, they would influence the hiring of other African Americans. The New Mexico Black Leadership Conference was designed as a catalyst to make this happen. Although we didn't keep statistics, I believe many doors were opened for African Americans using this approach. Even though many African Americans will not admit it, they were helped immensely by the work of the Conference.

We opened doors at Sandia Laboratories, and some African Americans were elevated to higher positions as a direct result of our actions. One of our members lost his job because of this push, but we were able to get him employment at the City of Albuquerque. We must realize that in the war against racism, there will always be casualties.

For over 25 years, I have been called in to conduct workshops on cultural awareness and diversity for the United States Department of Agriculture. I traveled across the nation working with employees in the Department. On August 8, 1974, I was scheduled to speak to all of the Under-Secretaries in the Department on the topic of cultural awareness. Prior to this day, there was a great deal of speculation about whether President Richard Nixon would resign. We were concerned about whether our workshop would go forward. This was truly a historic moment for our nation. Would government come to a standstill on that day? Surely a workshop on cultural awareness would lose its significance in the midst of such an important crisis involving the President.

Would all of the Under-Secretaries of the Department of Agriculture show or would their eyes be glued to the TV sets in their offices? Dr. John Aragon was one of the co-facilitators for the workshop and he and I made a gentle-man's bet. He felt that the seriousness of the situation and the gravity of the crisis almost assured the cancellation of the workshop. When we entered the meeting room, with one exception, all of the Under-Secretaries were in attendance. These were the highest-ranking officials in the Department, under the Secretary, Earl Butz. We wondered how this happened, even though we were pleasantly surprised. We could only conclude that it was Secretary Butz that had made it happen. He made a commitment to this effort. All of this happened before he put his foot in his mouth regarding African Americans. His statement was that all blacks want is an "indoor toilet, shoes that fit and a tight p_ _ _ _." His words certainly did not align with his actions.

We conducted the workshop in the midst of the resignation of the President of the United States of America. I was in Washington, the seat of power, when the person who held the most powerful position in the world stepped down from office. The transition of power that occurred could only happen in a few other places in the world. Being a history major in college, I could appreciate being in that place at that time.

During my five years at the University of New Mexico, I had the opportunity to meet many people whose presence added to the awareness and self-esteem of our campus and community. I was impressed by the poise of Angela Davis; the intelligence of Julian Bond; the openness of Charles Evers; the concern for children from Melba Moore; and the total commitment for black liberation of Stokely Carmichael, later known as Kwame Touré. These associations and my community activities brought investigators out of the woodwork. The FBI had, I assume still has, files on me, along with three files at the University of New Mexico, the State Police and the Albuquerque Police Department. I suspect that to this day I still continue to be the most investigated and scrutinized black man in New Mexico.

In 1973, I had been in the process of buying a house. I went down to the Credit Bureau to review my file. There was a strange code in the file, which was not familiar to the service person at the Bureau. Upon further inquiry (through a friend in the DA's office), I found out that the FBI had checked into my credit file. I wanted to know why, so I went to the FBI office and demanded to see the agent in charge. I was told that he was out of town and that he was the only one who could discuss the matter with me. I could never get in to see him. I wanted to know if it was legal for them to check my credit file. I eventually wrote the FBI office in Washington and requested a copy of my file under the Freedom of Information Act. The file that I received was quite extensive and very inaccurate.

During the early '70s and up to his death a few years ago, I developed a strong friendship with Kwame Touré (Stokely Carmichael). During his travels from coast to coast, he would often take an extra day or two and stay in my home to rest. He and I would sit and talk well into the night. He became very attached to my children and would always inquire as to how they were getting along. I saw a side of him that many people did not have the opportunity to observe. He was a man who was totally committed to changing the condition of black people throughout the world. He was the most unselfish man I have ever met. He never owned anything – no car, no house, no material things of value. He was an eloquent, well-known speaker, yet he was down to earth.

Kwame related a story to me that still sticks in my mind to this day. He and H. Rap Brown were in Mississippi with a group that was going to integrate an all-white school. He convinced one of the mothers to let them take her six year-old daughter to school. She told Kwame, "You take care of my little girl." He assured her that her daughter was in good hands. He held one of the little girl's hands and H. Rap Brown held the other. As they approached, a mob of white protesters had gathered, but they continued to walk toward the school. They could hear the name-calling, the yelling and screaming, but they still continued to approach the school. Then, someone from the mob threw a brick and it hit the little girl in the mouth. Kwame told me that from that moment he was never the same. That image continued to haunt him; I believe it haunted him until his death. I could detect a tremble in his voice when he talked about this incident. He felt responsible and he had a difficult time telling the mother what had happened to her little girl. He also said that H. Rap Brown evolved into a more militant activist as a result of what happened to this little girl.

Our paths continued to cross until Kwame moved to Africa. We lost direct communication. I was saddened when I learned he had prostate cancer. Later, I was deeply saddened when I received news of his death. He is sorely missed. His voice has been silenced, but his spirit lives on.

Time and circumstances have moved me into areas where I have forged friendships across many cultural lines; working relationships eventually turned into friendships. Working with Vicente Ximinez on the City of Albuquerque's Human Rights Board was a real learning experience for me. He could analyze an issue quicker than anyone I have known. Then he always seemed to have an answer that made sense. I would watch him work and would say, "Wow!" Having served under President Lyndon Johnson, Vicente Ximinez has forgotten more about civil rights than most people will ever know. He and I have developed a friendship that covers a span of 30 years.

During a march in Gallup, New Mexico, in 1975, I had the honor of marching alongside a great man who in due time became a great friend. Jose Rey Toledo was a Native American artist, storyteller and a man of peace. His wisdom will long be remembered. Activism comes with a great sacrifice, but it also comes with great rewards. Being able to call Jose Rey Toledo *friend* was one of those rewards.

The friendship that I experienced and enjoyed immensely was with Dr. John Aragon. We worked together at the University of New Mexico. We conducted cultural awareness workshops all across the United States together. I also taught classes for him at New Mexico Highlands University, when he served as President. We had numerous lunches together at the Barelas Coffee House, one of his favorite eating-places. We were together in Washington when President Nixon resigned. John was my hero and my mentor. He was a very intelligent man. The greatest symbol of our friendship was when he asked me to perform the wedding ceremony for his daughter. I accepted – it was a very special ceremony and a very special honor.

Some people hear the word *activist* and they think *problem.* I have been called an activist and I wear that label proudly, because I firmly believe that if there is no challenge, there will be no change.

Chapter VIII

Race and Politics New Mexico Style

During the latter part of May 1975, I received my Ph.D. from the University of New Mexico. It was a goal that I had set for myself and whatever it took, I was willing to pay the price and make the sacrifice. I felt that the time had come for me to shift gears and move into another direction. I felt that the time was right for me to move from the University of New Mexico setting because I was being typecast and I had essentially been ostracized. The old folks would say, *I had worn out my welcome.* I had challenged the system and won. There would be a price to pay. When the system mobilizes its resources against you the intent is to teach you a lesson. I remembered growing up and hearing the expression *payback is a b_ _ _ _.*

I had applied for another administrative position at UNM and I was in the final group of four. They interviewed the other three candidates, but failed to interview me. The standard procedure was that if an applicant made the final cut, he/she was supposed to be interviewed. There was no explanation given and I filed an internal grievance and prevailed. But, I saw the handwriting on the wall.

Shortly after that incident, an Anglo lady called me on the phone and indicated that she would like to make a donation to the Afro-American Studies Program. I told her that we would love to accept her donation and that she could make her check out to the University of New Mexico. She stated that she would prefer to donate cash. I told her that she could come by my office and I would accept the donation. When she arrived, I asked my secretary to come in to witness the transfer and type her a receipt. She stated that she did not want a receipt, left the money on my desk, and got up and walked out of the room.

To this day, I do not know who she was, but her actions did not pass the *smell* test. I took the cash over to the Cashier's Office, had it deposited in the Program's account, got a receipt and began to wonder, was I being set up? Had I not been able to account for those funds, I could have had criminal charges brought against me. From that moment on, I became extra cautious. I made sure that my car was locked at all times. I was not afraid that someone would steal something from my car, but that someone might place something *in* my car. Was I being paranoid or extra cautious? During those turbulent times, there were good reasons to be paranoid. I came to the conclusion that the time had come for me to move to another level.

Around the end of May 1975, my friend and Governor of the State, Jerry Apodaca, had been in office about four months. He offered me a position in his administration as Executive Director of the Governor's Council on Criminal Justice Planning. I resigned my position at the University of New Mexico and accepted the job in Santa Fe. I immediately became popular in the criminal justice community because I had money to give out in the form of grants. This popularity began to wane when I took the politics out of the grant-giving process. The emphasis was placed on the *little guy*, those small communities where a police car or a few extra dollars would make a big difference, rather than a large agency where a police car would be an *addition* to an existing fleet. This new process may not have been too popular, but it was fair and the small communities were helped immensely.

During those days, I was pretty naive about politics. Sure, I knew the politics of civil rights, confrontation and the politics of the streets, but State government in Santa Fe was a different ball game. The politics of the boardroom and the *Roundhouse* were a different challenge. The politics of negotiation, compromise, give and take, personal agendas and soothing egos was somewhat new to meI found out very quickly that if you did not learn and understand the game, a steamroller was right around the corner to flatten you out and teach you a lesson. If you got past the steamroller, there was a meat grinder waiting to chew you up and spit you out. In Santa Fe, you either play or you pay. This was a different world for me. I learned that everyone who smiled at you was not your friend. Some of the very people who shook your hand were prepared to rip it from the socket if they got the chance.

Working in Santa Fe was a great learning experience for me. I made a commitment to myself, however, that I would always stand up for my employees, no matter what the consequences. I also pledged that I would never play politics with the lives of other people. My people would always be protected.

These principles would be tested early in my position of Executive Director. Governor Apodaca had asked me to wear two hats. Mike Hanrahan had resigned as Director of the Department of Corrections, and in addition to my position as Executive Director, I was also asked to serve in that capacity until a new Director was brought on board.

The Corrections Commission ran the Department at that time, and essentially, the Director worked for them. At the first meeting of the Commission, I was called in and given a direct order to fire Felix Rodriguez, who had been Warden at the State Penitentiary and was now on staff in the central office of the Corrections Department. I did not even know Felix Rodriguez. I had no facts or any record of his job performance. I was told, "This is a direct order, fire Felix Rodriguez." I refused and informed the Commission that they had the authority to do so themselves. I was not about to fire a person without cause. I also did not want a firing to be my first official act in office.

The Chairman of the Commission took the matter to Governor Apodaca. The Governor called me to his office, and I thought my career in State government was over. I met with the Governor and explained the situation. Jerry Apodaca is a man of uncanny ability to analyze and size up situations and come to the right conclusions. He always backed his people, but he also held us accountable. I never knew him to micro-manage. He backed me in my decision to retain Felix Rodriguez. Although this was a decision I would later regret, at the time, it was the right thing to do. At the tail end of my conversation with Governor Apodaca, he asked me a question that still rings in my ears today, "Charles, are you sure about this?" My heart told me that retaining Felix was the right thing to do, but as I look back, my decision was very costly to the State of New Mexico and very damaging to me personally. He would later turn on me and join forces with those who sought to destroy me.

I served as Executive Director of the Governor's Council on Criminal Justice Planning until Governor Apodaca reorganized State government into 12 departments. He appointed me to be the Secretary of the Department of Criminal Justice. This was a bold move on his part because no African American had ever held such a high position in the State of New Mexico. What I admired most about Jerry was that he had courage. He could care less about what people said. He always did what he felt was right.

I recall when a small group of blacks went to see Jerry to try and talk him out of appointing me to the position of Cabinet Secretary. He told them that perhaps one of them should run for Governor the next time around. Then they could appoint whomever they pleased. But for now, as Governor, he would appoint who he wanted and that I was his man. He then ushered them out of his office. It was a real comfort to know that I not only had my boss' full support, I had his trust.

Governor Apodaca also empowered me to do my job. Shortly after he appointed me to his Cabinet, I drafted a list of "problems" facing the Department. There were about five or six items on my list. I made an appointment to meet with the

Governor and I presented my list of problems to him, asking him how he would like to have these problems dealt with. He looked at my list and asked, "Charles, how much do I pay you?" I told him what he already knew. His reply was, "Each of these look like a $5,000 decision. If I have to make these decisions for you, then why do I need you?" I picked up my list and his final words were, "Don't bring me problems, bring me solutions." He had empowered me to run my department. This reflected his style of management. Governor Apodaca would let you do your job, but he also held you accountable.

Early in his administration, Jerry would be tested by an incident that occurred at the Employment Security Commission. An African American, by the name of Gusundi, took over the building and barricaded himself inside on one of the floors. No one knew very much about this man, but apparently he had tried to get a job with the State and something went wrong. He demanded more jobs for African Americans in State government, and he demanded a meeting with the Governor. I advised Jerry that it would not be a good idea for him to meet with this man. I was not concerned for the Governor's safety; I was concerned about Gusundi's safety. Jerry would have probably kicked his rear end until he couldn't lift his foot anymore.

Jerry and I agreed that I would meet with Gusundi. I set up a meeting and we had quite a conversation. Some of what he said was hard to understand, but he appeared to be quite sincere about wanting more employment for African Americans. We started our conversation on shaky ground because he didn't know who I was, and I felt uneasy with him because I didn't know his background. He did not volunteer much information about his past. He wanted to know why he couldn't meet with the Governor and I was quite frank with him. I explained that he had taken over a State building. Under any other circumstances, a meeting with the Governor might be possible, but we would be setting a dangerous precedent if he met with him under these circumstances. Whenever someone wanted to meet with the Governor, they could take over a building and demand a meeting. I let him know that I had the Governor's ear and that his voice would be heard, but only through me.

I did not know what this guy was thinking. He never smiled, nor did he change his facial expression. We were meeting late at night in a house in the Northeast Heights and no one knew where I was. There was a long pause and he finally spoke. He said, "Okay, I understand." I thought, *Thank you Lord!*

I met with Jerry and proposed to him that he appoint a task force on black employment and concentrate on recruitment and placement. He agreed and we were able to bring several African Americans into State government. Gusundi disappeared, but he surfaced several years later in San Francisco, where he took over another building.

Two of my biggest antagonists during my time under Governor Apodaca were Martin Vigil, Chief of the State Police, and Mahlon Love, Chairman of the State Police Board. When the State Police were placed under my supervision, Martin refused to answer my phone calls or come to my office for meetings. He could not face the realization that he no longer reported to the Governor, but to me. I believe being black was a factor, but also being a civilian compounded the problem. I knew that this was an issue I had to correct. I did not want to take this to the Governor because this was my battle and I had to fight it, and win. Martin did not have to like me, but he had to show respect for the position that I held and work with me for the good of the entire Department.

While reviewing budgets for each division in my department, I discovered a very interesting line item in the State Police budget. The line item was for subsistence pay for State Police officers. This pay was designed to help officers who had to travel the highways and could not go home for meals. I found out that *all* State police officers were receiving this extra compensation, even the high paid officials in Santa Fe, who did very little travel. I asked Chief Vigil to justify why those officials who made high salaries, did very little travel, and took their meals at home, qualified for subsistence pay. He came by my office with the memo in his hand and we had a good discussion about the matter. We made an agreement that I would leave the subsistence pay in the budget in exchange for his cooperation. We got along fine after that. Martin made the choice to call a truce, if only for the moment. I knew that the fight had been delayed, but would be fought at another time.

Martin and I had another encounter during the tail end of the Apodaca administration. Lieutenant Governor Bob Ferguson and Former Governor Bruce King were locked in a struggle to represent the Democratic Party as the candidate for governor in the primary election, and both had attended a political rally in the Los Lunas area. Due to the location of the rally, cars had to be parked in one area and attendees had to walk about a half mile to the rally area. Bob Ferguson was walking to the area and a State police car passed him by with Bruce King sitting in the back seat. King was being driven to the rally area, while a State-elected Lieutenant Governor walked.

I called Martin into my office. He *hated* to be called to my office. I asked him about this incident and he verified the report. I told him that I did not feel that a State Police vehicle should be used to transport political candidates, but if he did it for one, he should do it for the other. Martin was livid. I asked him who authorized the action. (I knew that very little went on in that department that Martin did not know about). He stated that there was no preplanning on anyone's part. The officer spotted Bruce King and offered to drive him to the site of the rally. They did not see Bob Ferguson, or they would have extended the same courtesy. As far as I was concerned, this ended the matter. Martin indicated to me that Bruce King was going to be our next governor and "when he comes in all this is going to change." The ink was in the well and the handwriting was on the wall. A big political and unfortunately, racial battle was looming on the horizon.

Martin Vigil was not my only challenge. Clyde Malley, Warden at the State Penitentiary, was cut from the same ego cloth. He also resented having to report to me. I am not sure if Clyde had anything to do with this or not, but I know that some of the State Pen employees used to refer to me as "Leroy" and "the nigger upstairs." The atmosphere at the State Pen was not good because the warden had set up an adversarial relationship of *us against them.* They wanted to continue to operate independent of the Department. For years, the penitentiary had operated as a private system, with very little accountability to anyone.

My goal was that all the Criminal Justice divisions cooperate so that we could have a unified department. Since there was so much resistance, I had to find a way to manage all of the entities for which I was responsible. I knew that if I got control of the budget, I could get the cooperation I needed. One of the worst things that can happen to a manager in any organization is to be held accountable for a program that he/she has no control over. Since I had to submit a department budget, Corrections had to submit their budget to me for approval. I held department budget hearings, and each division head had to justify every line item and make a case for any increases. If the Warden refused, then the State Pen budget would be submitted based on existing figures, or figures I had chosen.

As I reviewed the budget for Corrections, I found some discrepancies I considered to be quite serious. Monies were coming into Corrections that did not come through the State system. Separate accounting and disbursement systems were utilized, and there was no way to tell how much money came in or where the money went. As I began to take control of the budget, the resistance intensified. The more I questioned some of the *hidden* items in the existing budget, the more "Leroy" I became. When you push the system, at some point the system will push back!

Perhaps the only time that Governor Apodaca and I disagreed philosophically was when the Determinate Sentencing Bill hit his desk. I urged the Governor to veto the bill. I was concerned that this law would increase the prison population, which in turn would increase the need for more facilities and staff, plus increase security concerns. I felt that the bill was passed by the Legislature based on emotion, with little thought about how it would impact the system. Jerry sensed the mood of the Legislature and he told me that "this is what the people want." As he traveled throughout the State and listened to the citizens, he heard them say they wanted longer sentences and they wanted flat sentences. This is what we got and I still feel we took the wrong direction. I believe that a flat sentence increased our security risk, increased our costs, and developed an overcrowding problem. As we began to look at expansion, we developed a Corrections Master Plan. We renovated an existing facility at Los Lunas and initiated a proposal for a medium security facility at the same site.

Then we bought the old Villa Solano building on the outskirts of Roswell. The building was renovated using inmate labor. Roswell was initiated as a facility where inmates were required to work and, in turn, pay for their own room, board and transportation. Consequently, this facility has paid for itself many times over.

We were also faced with a very serious legal situation; we had female inmates in a facility on the same grounds as juveniles, and a 1973 federal court decision ruled that women had to be afforded the same opportunities for rehabilitation as men. We were in contempt of court. The law required sight and sound separation of children and adults. We could not build a women's prison. We had no money, no time and no commitment from the Legislature. We looked for suitable space all over the State but nothing was available. The pressure to solve this problem with no money for construction was quite intense. A temporary solution was found at Radium Springs.

Since this was a former resort, many people felt that these inmates were taking hot baths from the underground springs every day and enjoying the good life. This was not the case. This site had had opposition from the start. The feeling was, *place them somewhere, but not there.* With most communities saying this, the options were quite limited. The women were moved to Radium Springs. This move forced the State to evaluate the need for a women's prison and eventually pass legislation to build one.

I enjoyed my tenure as Cabinet Secretary under Jerry Apodaca immensely. I enjoyed making tough decisions and working with and supervising some of the finest people in state government. Many of them supported me. However, my staff did understand that if I made*one* mistake, the press would be on me like ugly on an ape. I told them that if I made that mistake, I would not be treated like the other Cabinet Secretaries. I was a story and one mistake, even the perception of a mistake, would be news. Sadly, this has been the case with most blacks who have held high positions in government. Joe Johnson, Cabinet Secretary under Governor Anaya, was investigated and almost sent to jail. Lenton Malry was accused of wrong doings in the Human Rights Office. Marsha Hardeman is another example, and of course, yours truly. As African Americans get closer to the top, we become bigger targets for the system.

I learned at an early age that there are dual standards – two sets of rules; one set for blacks and another set for whites. That's the way it is. That's the way it has always been, and I suspect that's the way it will *always* be.

My intentions were to leave state government at the end of the Apodaca administration, when Jerry left office. I knew that a new governor would be taking office in January, 1979, and if the Republican candidate, Joe Skeen, won he would bring in his own people. If Bruce King, the Democrat candidate, won he had a right to appoint his own people also. After all, I had supported King's opponent in the primary. I had no plans, but I had a few weeks to work on something.

During the second week of October, prior to the general election, I was working in my office when I received a call from Ben Alexander, a prominent Democrat and a good friend, calling from his office in Hobbs. He was on his speakerphone. Ben told me that David King, Bruce King's nephew, was in his office. David said, "Hello." I said, "Hello" and began to wonder about the phone call. Ben explained that the polls showed that the race for governor was too close to call. He stated that the response from the black community statewide was lukewarm, at best. Ben stated that they needed my help because they needed the black vote. Many of my friends statewide were holding back on their decisions on who they would vote for because they did not know what was going to happen to me. Would I retain my position or would I be replaced?

Until that day in October of the election year, I had not heard from the King camp. Now they were asking for my help. I came to the realization that even though the black community is small in numbers, we can make a difference in a close election. We had demonstrated that before, when Jerry Apodaca ran for governor and won. I told Ben and David that I was not really focused on this election. Besides, I had word that Bruce was still upset with me because of the Bob Ferguson affair, when I reprimanded Martin Vigil for giving him a ride and passing by Lieutenant Governor Bob Ferguson.

Then David dropped an unexpected bombshell. "Charles, if you help us and we win the election, we will re-appoint you to your position on the Cabinet." I asked David if Bruce was in agreement with this proposition. He said that he was speaking on behalf of Bruce King. This sounded like a fair arrangement to me, a win/win situation for us both. I campaigned hard for Bruce King, and I know that the black community contributed significantly to his victory.

When it was announced that I was going to be re-appointed as Secretary of the Department of Criminal Justice, I clearly remember a question asked by a reporter for the *Albuquerque Journal*, "Charles, are you ready for this?" Little did I know that his question was a warning of things that would happen to me over the next year.

After the appointment notification, I ran into Senator Manny Aragon, and he asked me if I knew that there was an effort being made to block my confirmation and that it would be a good idea if I talked to some of the Senators and lined up some support. I did not know where the opposition was coming from, so I began to ask questions. Joe Romero, one of my employees, came into my office and told me that he had been at a function where Governor King was present. He said that he had complimented the Governor on my appointment and the Governor responded,

"He has not been confirmed yet." I still had not figured out where the opposition was coming from. I made an appointment to see the Governor, and I told him that if he wanted someone else for this position, all he had to do was let me know. He assured me three times that he wanted me to serve in his administration.

Then things started to get crazy! I started getting blasted in the newspapers. First of all, Dorothy King attacked me and her comments were printed in newspapers all over the State of New Mexico. She said that she opposed my confirmation because I was "too liberal." I had never met this woman before; I had never seen her before, nor had she ever been to my department. Who was she? She was the Governor's sister-in-law! Two and two always equals four – I knew that she would not speak without permission from Bruce King. I came to the conclusion that the opposition was coming from my boss.

I realized that I was about to engage in the fight of my life. Was I prepared to fight this kind of battle? Should I have also read something into the fact that my appointment was the next to the last to be confirmed? Should I leave? I was confused. The Governor had told me that he wanted me to serve in his administration. *Why is this happening to me?* Senators Caleb Chandler and Ken Schleintz joined Dorothy King in the attack. Their contention was that I was not qualified for a job that I had been already doing for two years. I discussed this situation with my trusted staff. They convinced me to fight through this and assured me that I had their full support. I had never waged war against my own boss before, but now was the time to re-focus my efforts. I could not lose my competitive edge. This was not just a fight for a job – it was a fight for my dignity; the job became secondary.

My good friend and a man of unquestionable integrity, Fred McCaffrey, wrote an article on Wednesday, February 14, 1979, in the *New Mexican Opinion* that really summed up the whole situation quite well. The article read:

Political game snares Becknell

> To understand politics – and politicians – you sometimes have to mull over the way events fit together. Here's one such pattern that emerges from recent news.
>
> Event No. 1: Bruce King is running for governor, in what he realizes with horror is going to be a very tight race, which he could conceivably lose despite the voting strength of the Democratic party. He seeks help, of any kind, wherever he can find it.

Event No. 2: An offer of help with voters in Hobbs and other communities with black constituencies comes from the father of Charles Becknell, Jerry Apodaca's Cabinet Secretary for Criminal Justice. The candidate presumably accepts the offer with alacrity.

Event No. 3: The voters go to the polls and elect Bruce King governor by a slim margin, 174,631 votes to Joe Skeen's 170,848. The King forces sigh happily; they have pulled off a squeaker, but a victory all the same.

Event No. 4: Post-election analysis credits the Becknells' work with helping to hold King's losing margin in Lea county to about a thousand votes and with strong voter turnout for King in black precincts across the state. Shortly thereafter, the governor-elect announces he is renaming Charles Becknell to his cabinet position.

Event No. 5: Reporters conferring with Becknell after his reappointment ask him what he will do if King insists he fire John Ramming and Giovanni Greco, rehabilitated ex-convicts who hold high positions in his department. Both are known to be strongly resented by the State Police, placed under Becknell in state government reorganization. Becknell says, "*I'll resign.*"

Event No. 6: Becknell's reappointment meets stiff but unsuccessful opposition in both Senate Rules and on the floor. He is confirmed by a 30-11 vote, but not till after one senator hints broadly, on the record, that Governor King has garnered votes for confirmation by promising Senators that Becknell will be gone from the job in six months or less. Implication is that the confirmation process is, in that event, nothing more than a hollow charade.

Event No. 7: Governor King tells reporters there is "a strong possibility" that Ramming and Greco, whose presence makes him want to remove the State Police from Becknell's control, will be removed from their jobs.

Sometimes governing a state is as complex, and as fascinating, as a chess game.

Governor King got the election-day help he needed and paid his debt, as black voters must admit, by continuing Becknell in his job. But when Becknell, out of loyalty, tied his continuation in office to the presence of Ramming and Greco, he played into his enemies' hands.

Now all the Governor has to do is insist that they be fired, and those who want Becknell's demise, most notably the State Police and their supporters, get Becknell's head on a platter.

One little move here…one little move there…and checkmate: It's not statecraft at the level of a Medici court or as practiced in the Vatican; but in our crude New Mexican manner, it's equally real.

What's sad is that the chess pieces in this kind of game are men, not wood – and men can bleed.

On Tuesday, February 6, 1979, I sat before the Senate Rules Committee in Room 319 of the Roundhouse, as the New Mexico State Capitol Building is called. A few days before, I had been made aware of the fact that my confirmation as Cabinet Secretary of the Criminal Justice Department was in trouble. Allegedly, one of the Senators on the Rules Committee had collected enough evidence and lined up enough votes to block my confirmation.

I looked around me and the room was packed – mostly with friends, but also by a few curiosity seekers and members of the press. At that moment I knew that my entire life – my whole professional future – was on the line. For many years, more than I can remember, I stood alone and fought my own battles, but I knew that this was one fight that I could not fight and win on my own. I needed the help of friends. Senator Harry McAdams, a fellow Hobbsan and a man who believed the situation was unfair, presented me to the Committee. As he spoke to the Committee about my childhood days in Hobbs, and about my educational pursuits and how I eventually obtained my Ph.D. from the University of New Mexico, my mind began to wander. I was suddenly jolted into a brutal reality – the reality that I was a black man heading up one of the most powerful and certainly the most conservative department in the State of New Mexico.

As my mind continued to wander, in brief intervals I began to assess just how I got to this particular place and time in history. Usually, when I am faced with difficult decisions to make, or when I am confronted with tense and difficult situations, I begin my approach by thinking of something beautiful. On this particular day, I closed my eyes briefly and I saw a rainbow – a huge, beautiful rainbow with many colors. In my mind, those things that contain beauty also contain the truth. That day, I was seeking some answers about myself and about what it meant to be black in New Mexico – I was seeking the truth.

As my friends began to testify, they were telling the members of the Rules Committee that I was a good person, with solid family roots and that I was a man of integrity. But when Senator Kenneth Schleintz, a Republican from Tucumcari, began to speak and interrogate me, I knew that my moral character and my managerial capabilities were not important. Then I began to focus in on what I was really prepared to defend, my administrative abilities. I felt that if this was the issue, I would win hands down because I had built a reputation as a competent administrator. The rainbow became more radiant and I was inspired by that beautiful multi-colored symbol of beauty and truth. I was ready for war, because I had the truth on my side. But then Senator Schleintz said, "Dr. Becknell, I want you to know that what I am about to say to you is not racial," (he had just played the race card). "I am not prejudiced, because my wife's best friend is a black gal." I knew then that I would not be fighting the same battle as my white colleagues. At that moment, I knew that my battle would be a racial one. The deck was stacked, my back was against the wall and Senator Schleintz held the trump card.

My rainbow disappeared and I felt helpless because I had no defense for this kind of battle. I was not prepared for this kind of fight. I have fought prejudice and racism all my life, but it was usually for someone else. The racism I fought in my lifetime was usually subtle, but this was different, because I was in an open forum with the TV cameras zooming down on me for all the State to see. I repeatedly had to face those open racial attacks by members of the Senate Rules Committee

I sat calmly as Senator Schleintz continued his attack and I began to evaluate my thinking; several questions came to mind. *Am I in Mississippi or in New Mexico?* Certainly, had I been in Mississippi I probably would have been treated better because there is an unwritten code of conduct for black/white relations. The other question that came to mind was one that I did not want to attempt to answer, but I had to answer if I was to defend myself. Therefore, I asked myself, *Why is this happening to me? Is this race or politics?* To fight a battle you need to know and understand the battle you are fighting.

Being a historian, I began to internalize the infamous words of Abraham Lincoln during the Lincoln-Douglass debate:

> "I will say then that I am not, nor ever have been, in favor of bringing about in any way the social and political equality of the white and black races; and I am not, nor ever have been, in favor of making voters or jurors of Negroes, nor of qualifying them to hold office, nor to intermarry with white people;

> and I will say, in addition to this that there is a physical difference between the white and black races which I believe will forever forbid the two races from living together on equal terms of social and political equality. And inasmuch as they cannot so live while they do remain together there must be a position of superior and inferior, and I as much as any other man am in favor of having the superior position assigned to the white race."

I had been an administrator in New Mexico State government since May of 1975. From 1975 until my hearing before the Rules Committee, with the exception of one Senator, many members of the Legislature had treated me with dignity and respect. For four years I was able to function normally as an agency head because I had the support of my boss, Jerry Apodaca. Yet, I knew that there were many subtle pressures on me because of being the first and only black administrator. I stood out and was constantly under scrutiny. This inescapable reality made my job extremely difficult. To survive as a black administrator of a criminal justice system that included the State Police was an amazing feat in itself. I had to walk a tight rope in attempting to develop and maintain a working relationship with individuals and factions whose ideas were basically incompatible with mine.

As I continued to try and answer Senator Schleintz's loaded questions, I again began to reflect on certain events in my life that had led me to this hearing. With the exception of about three years, all of my life had been spent in New Mexico. I have a right to be here and to be a part of the governmental process. But, as I listened to Senator Schleintz's personal attacks, I began to wonder, *Where does a black man go in this state for respect if not to our state's capitol? Where is a black man safe in this state if not on the Senate floor?*

In every job I have taken on, I have tried to do well and to the best of my abilities; but of more importance, I have always attempted to excel. I have always tried to do a job *better* than anyone else would have done it. I was very hurt by the barrage of attacks that I was receiving from the Senator, especially when he emphatically stated that I was incompetent.

As stated before, I was painfully aware of the reality that I had one major mistake to make, whether real or invented. Even as I write these words today, that statement is still a fact. Since no black person had ever held such a high position before, the feeling prevailed that we were not competent enough to do the job; and the skeptics were always waiting for that one big error. Knowing this placed me under a great deal of pressure because one error in judgment could end my career. To prevent this judgment error, it was imperative that I learn as much as possible about the organization, both administratively and politically, and surround myself with loyal, competent people. Even with this combination, the pressure was tremendous.

The other side of the pressure coin comes in relating to the black community. At last they finally had someone they could relate to in a position of power. Being a visible symbol of black achievement and a friendly contact person, I became the black community's source of contact with state government. Even if the matters did not relate to the criminal justice area, I was expected to solve all their problems. Some of my colleagues viewed my inquiries on behalf of my black constituency as interference. OnceI was even accused of trying to influence decisions because I tried to get answers for a citizen who happened to be black. The immediate reaction on the part of these non-black agency heads was that I was helping this individual because I was getting something on the side.

Perhaps the most frustrating problem I have encountered as a black administrator has been the illusion of power that a high level black official projects to the black community. I have been expected to perform miracles simply because I was a member of the Governor's Cabinet. The black community assumed that I had a thousand jobs in my hip pocket and that I could pass these jobs out on demand. When a black person expressed an interest to me about a particular job and I could not deliver on that job, even though it was in a different department, I was not being responsive to the needs of the black community. If I was successful in helping one person get a job, then others felt I could do the same for them, and if I did not produce for them, it was because I was unconcerned or I had sold out (an Uncle Tom). This view is summed up by Professor Stuart Taylor of the Harvard Business School in a study of black executives with similar problems who reports:

> "The black executive's corporate life is very lonely, indeed. Considered an Uncle Tom by many blacks and a 'nigger' by many whites, he is the nigger in the middle."

I have always been aware that my survival in state government depended on the black constituency because if one is to survive in the political arena, he must have a base of support. Therefore, any evaluation of my job performance had to include how well I helped my black constituency in their dealings with a very complex bureaucracy. The complexity intensifies when one realizes that as a black administrator I was confronted by the same problems, the same policies that any other black person had. My only advantage was that I had greater access to the power structure than any other black person. I had to learn to deal intimately with the white power structure and all of its complex, and sometimes exclusive, policies plus the inner realities of the black world as well. For survival sake, I could not completely separate myself from either world.

The other major frustration that I have had to live with was that any accomplishments made in the Department were always made by *someone* else. The usual comments were, *Well, he could not have done it if he didn't have Joe Blow on his staff*, or *He's just a figurehead. His staff does all the work.* Finally, *He really doesn't know what he is doing, his staff leads him around.* As stated earlier, I found it necessary to surround myself with a good staff. In fact, I wanted the best people – those who would question things and pose new, creative ideas. They were hired on their abilities as technicians. I felt that it was my job to tell them what I wanted, so as to provide leadership and direction. As technicians, they were to put the ideas together into a viable program. We were very successful with this approach. I always gave credit to my staff for their efforts and accomplishments.

I can vividly recall an incident that occurred on a trip to Farmington, New Mexico, in 1977. I had a scheduled meeting there and I took three of my staff members along. We had previously arranged to be picked up at the airport. The person who was there to pick us up had never seen me before, so when we got off the plane, she walked up to one of my white staff members and extended her hand as she welcomed "Dr. Becknell to Farmington." My staff member was quite embarrassed because he knew the racial implications. He politely withdrew his hand and stated, "I am not Dr. Becknell," and he pointed in my direction and said, "he is." The lady turned red and immediately began to apologize for her obvious mistake.

The struggle for recognition and acceptance is perhaps the most difficult struggle for any black person in New Mexico. Due to the fact that the numbers of blacks have always been small, little recognition has been given to blacks in New Mexico. Much to the displeasure of many blacks, New Mexico is still regarded as a tri-cultural state: a concept that embraces the Anglo, Spanish and Native American communities. This concept ignores the presence of blacks and the many contributions that they have made to the state of New Mexico.

So, again, as I assessed my confirmation struggle and the strong racial undercurrents involved, I began to ask myself, *Is it worth it? Why not tell them to "stick it" and walk away?* Then I thought, *Charles Becknell walking away from a fight? Never! No challenge, no change.* But at this point in my life I was ready to do so. I felt that if they wanted my job, they could take it and shove it. But I could never allow them to take away my dignity – this was a fight for my dignity.

The day after the hearing before the Rules Committee, I went into my office and shut the door. I said a brief prayer and began to ponder my resignation. I wanted to draft my letter in such a way that I could resign with dignity. As I pondered over the wording, one of my staff members came in to talk to me. She inquired about my plans for lunch. Having none, we decided to go to the Palace Restaurant and discuss the whole situation.

During lunch, this staff member convinced me that there was no way I could gracefully bow out of this one. The timing was too critical and there would be more to lose by leaving than by staying. There were a number of new programs on the drawing board; the Department was in a state of confusion because most of my time was being spent on everything except administrative matters. At this most critical period, when my staff really needed me, I could not provide them with the leadership they needed because I was fighting for my personal and professional life. I could see things gradually deteriorating, yet, there was very little I could do.

At the same time, I was faced with numerous personal problems, and it did not help that my spiritual life was in shambles. It appeared that at this time that the vultures came out, the sharks were circling in the waters and everyone wanted a piece of my soul. Staff morale was down; some staff members were knifing me in the back. The Governor was playing games with my life, and the press was having a field day at my expense. This was a very difficult time for me. Prayer was my only comfort.

At this point, I did not know which way to turn, or who to turn to. The major question was *Which battle do I fight first?*

I spent a great deal of time in solitude because the answers did not come easily. I knew that I had some major decisions to make and they had to be made soon. Every second, every minute, was quite crucial. As I often do in difficult situations, I prayed to God for guidance. I was directed to Psalm 121:1,2a

> "I will lift up mine eyes to the hills,
> from whence cometh my help.
> My help cometh from the Lord."

I began to feel as though I was no longer alone. I decided to stay and fight, because I concluded that I had more going for me than against me. I felt as though I had a partner with me that nobody could touch. It was analogous to having the toughest kid on the block as your best friend. So I felt that the odds were in my favor. I was also directed to Proverbs 16:9

"A man's heart deviseth his way:
but the Lord directeth his steps."

I decided to pursue this battle one step at a time – one day at a time – because I felt that time was on my side. Every day I came to the office, I prayed to God and repeated over and over, "I can do all things through Christ which strengtheneth me." (Philippians 4:13)

On the basis of faith in God and a renewed faith in myself, I waged my battle to defend my dignity. I knew that there could be no real winner in this battle because whoever won would possess a shallow victory.

The battle took its toll on me personally, and it pointed out many things that are still going through my mind to this day.

First of all, I found out quickly who my friends were. My friends immediately came to my defense. Those who could not come, called to see if I was all right and offered words of encouragement. My other *friends* were not really sure if the accusations made against me were true or not, so they just waited in the wings until the storm blew over. Once it was over, they called and said, "I was with you all the way."

Throughout the whole ordeal, there were many disappointments, but none that could match the fact that some of my own people, some people from the black community, actually contributed to my misery. Also disappointing was the fact that some of the members of the State Senate for whom I had a lot of respect really showed their true *colors* and used me as a political football on the Senate floor.

Finally, there were some members of the media who stuck by me and reported the events in a balanced way. On the other hand were the ambitious journalists who were looking to make a name for themselves, at my expense.

My children suffered from all of the publicity surrounding the confirmation battle. Because my name and picture were all over the news I remember my ten-year-old son asking me if I was in trouble and if I was going to jail. It was extremely difficult for me to explain to him what the whole matter was about; I didn't completely understand it myself.

I sat nervously on the Senate platform. As Senator Schleintz spoke I could see the pain and anguish in the eyes of Lieutenant

Governor Roberto Mondragon, who was presiding over the Senate. I could sense that he was bleeding, just as I was. I sat and waited and waited for them to get to the vote. I kept asking, *God, when will this all end?*

After what seemed like an eternity, the Chairman called for the confirmation vote on my position as Cabinet Secretary of Criminal Justice:

Alarid	Yes	Lee	Yes
Altamirano	Yes	Leger	Yes
Aragon	Yes	Martinez	Yes
Becht	No	McAdams	Yes
Chandler	No	Mercer	No
Chavez, Tito	Yes	Montoya	Absent
Chavez, Willie	Absent	Morgan	Yes
Conway	No	Morrow	Yes
Dunn	Yes	Lopez	Yes
Eoff	No	Olguin	Yes
Fidel	Yes	Papen	Yes
Gant	Yes	Pinto	Yes
Goodell	Yes	Rogers	Yes
Gurule	Yes	Rutherford	Yes
Gwaltney	Yes	Schleintz	No
Hansen	Yes	Sitta	No

Houston	Yes	Smalley	No
Irick	Yes	Thompson	Yes
Jennings	No	Trujillo	Yes
King	Yes	Valentine	No
Lang	Yes	Wood	No

I was confirmed. Eleven Senators voted against me, but of more importance, 29 voted in favor. I was relieved. But also, I was ashamed of my state and the legislative process. I felt that the New Mexico State Senate had been less than dignified that day. When all of this was over, I walked away from the Senate platform with my head held high; I walked out as a man. I immediately walked behind the Senate gallery and found a quiet, secluded spot. I thanked God, then I cried. I cried alone.

An article written by John Robertson appeared in the *Santa Fe New Mexican* stating that Senator Schleintz claimed he was told that I would be dismissed by Governor King within six months. He is quoted as asking some of his fellow Senators, "How many of you have been told to go ahead and vote for him because he is going to be let go in six months?" Senator Aubrey Dunn also stated on the Senate floor, "If the Governor does not want this man, he should tell him and not leave this to us." Sometimes you don't have to kick the system for it to kick you. However, if adversity does not kill you, it should make you stronger. It should make you better – not bitter. I had taken on the Governor of the State of New Mexico. Even though I had won the confirmation, the system was not giving up - it was gearing up to deliver another assault.

I was presented with some very damaging information about one of my antagonists in the State Senate. I chose not to use it because I would have to sink to his level. I will take that information to my grave. Besides, the Lord said, "Vengeance is mine and I will repay." No doubt this man eventually suffered more than I had.

About 12 years later, I received a call from Senator Schleintz's wife. She had been trying to reach me for several weeks. She informed me that the Senator had passed away, but before he died he asked her to find me and tell me that he was sorry for what he put me through and asked for my forgiveness. I told her that I was sorry he had passed and that he had been forgiven a long time ago. Tears came to my eyes because an unfortunate chapter in my life had been closed.

Even though the attacks on me were public, the closure was private. Perhaps that is the way God intended things to be. Two men from two different worlds found peace. Not on the battlefield but in the heart: a private matter between two men who found a mutual place of honor. I have found over the years that there is dignity and peace in forgiveness. The love of God, as well as peace and understanding, can be found in those individuals who ask for and extend forgiveness.

A few years earlier, Mahlon Love had explained to me that his involvement in the effort to discredit me was not personal, but to get the State Police removed from under my supervision. I took that as a veiled apology. Perhaps the reason for the attacks against me were designed to get the State Police removed from under my authority and the race card was played to make this happen. Mahlon Love told me, "It was not personal." The sad part about all of this is that things did not have to happen the way they did. The Governor could have removed the State Police with the stroke of a pen. I suppose vilification always makes unpleasant deeds seem justifiable.

When I forgave all of my tormentors, the world looked a little brighter and I no longer had to carry around anger and animosity in my heart. A tremendous weight was lifted from my shoulders. I could then look ahead with clarity. I became a much stronger person because I had come through a major battle. Everything else would be a minor skirmish – so I led myself to believe. I later came to realize that if you are African American in New Mexico and you travel in circles reserved for an elite few, you essentially have a target on your back and a price on your head. Senator Les Houston once stated publicly that he would have my head on a silver platter.

The next onslaught I had to contend with was a management review of my department. Frank Kleinhenz was hired to conduct the review. I assume the reason for the review was due to the allegations of incompetence leveled against me by Senator Schleintz, but ordered by Governor King. The review did not reveal any major problems.

Then the process of dismantling the department began. The State Police was removed from the Department and the Corrections Training Academy was dismantled; who was in charge of the Department now became confusing. It soon became clear that Felix Rodriguez, Joanne Brown, Bud Richards and Governor King were now in charge. I became a figurehead. Was it time to go? I talked to some of my key staff people. Since the confirmation battle had been won, maybe it was time to go. My staff convinced me that we had too many good programs going and some still on the drawing board for me to leave. They told me that we could fight through this current situation and assured me that I had their full support.

I listened to them. Perhaps, I should have listened to my heart, but it is hard to leave when the job is unfinished. I decided to see how things would play out, but my department began to disintegrate before my eyes. The system was kicking back. I began to realize that the strategy was to punish me by removing programs from under my authority until there would be very little left for me to manage. Then, the end result would be to get me to resign.

After the management audit of my department, conducted by Frank Kleinhenz, was completed David King, Secretary of the Department of Finance and Administration (DFA), called me to his office. He was quite concerned about our budget request for approximately 33 new correctional officers. The Corrections Department had just renovated and expanded the Los Lunas Minimum Security facility and due to this expansion, we needed additional personnel. He pointed out to me that the Governor had made a campaign promise that there would be no new positions in state government.

We had a problem – we had a *big* problem. I stood my ground and pushed for these new employees because we had to maintain a certain level of security and we did not have enough personnel to even cover existing needs. Without my input and upon the recommendation of Felix Rodriguez, the request was deleted and correction officer positions were shifted from existing facilities to the new facility at Los Lunas. That meant facilities that were already understaffed and had positions they could not fill or were in the process of filling, lost those positions. The State Peitentiary was the hardest hit, but the impact was devastating at Camp Sierra Blanca.

As I look back, I wonder how I could have been so naïve; all of the events that led up to this time should have slapped me in the face. I should have realized that I was not only an outsider, but an outsider on borrowed time. That six-month commitment made by Governor King that I would be gone should have been a wakeup call. I sincerely believed that I could straighten things out and earn his trust through good works and making sound decisions. However, when I would go over to the fourth floor of the Capitol building, and walk past the Governor's office and see one of my employees, Felix Rodriguez, waiting outside to see the Governor, I should have known that Corrections' policy was not in my hands. Felix Rodriguez and Governor King were now running the department. The responsibility had been removed from my hands, but not the blame.

Another player entered the picture by the name of Bud Richards from Las Cruces. Bud was Chairman of the Corrections Advisory Commission. Once Bruce King came into office, Bud began giving me instructions, prefaced with, "I have cleared this with the Governor" or "The Governor and I agreed." I was expected to follow the directives of a citizen appointee who resided in Las Cruces and I probably saw once a month.

I objected once about how he gave his instructions. I told him that this is not a plantation and I was not a field hand. His tone was demeaning and I drew the line. Tom Day, a *Journal* reporter, wrote an article saying that I called Bud Richards a racist. I believe that that was the headline. I questioned Tom about that and asked him for proof that I made that comment. His response was "Well, you certainly implied it." Racist is not a term that I use lightly. I asked him to correct this error, but it never happened. Shortly thereafter, Brian Sanderoff, one of Bruce King's assistants, called me into his office and told me that the Governor asked him to talk to me because it appeared as though I was "out of control." He informed me that Bud Richards represented the Governor and I had to work with him. My question was, "Do I have to work for him?" That was a challenge and now was the time to gear up for the next assault.

In November 1979, an incident occurred at Camp Sierra Blanca that had a rippling effect throughout the entire state. Two inmates got into a fight, and I believe others joined in. They had been drinking and this intensified the situation. One inmate was killed, and a Corrections officer was hurt and found tied up. There were only two officers on duty, and the other officer who found the hurt one could not take him for treatment because the facility would be left unsecured. He could only call for another officer on staff to come. They had to wait until he got dressed and showed up to relieve them before they could get help for the injured officer. I believe the position that was eliminated from this facility would have made a difference in the response time to this incident.

The inmates at this facility were considered minimum security. They would go into town every day and work, then return to the facility in the evening. Due to a shortage of staff, trusted inmates drove the van to drop others off and pick them up. They were pretty much under an honor system. This particular evening, one of the inmates bought, or somehow obtained, a bottle of liquor. The van stopped about a half-mile from the facility and they hid the bottle. When they arrived at the facility, they were searched, but after bed check, one of the inmates slipped out, got the bottle and the drinking started. The drinking was eventually followed by the violence.

An official and irresponsible statement came out of the Governor's office that stated that certain inmates at the minimum security facilities would be brought back to the State Penitentiary for re-evaluation. Inmates who had a *snitch* jacket on them looked upon this statement as a death sentence. They couldn't go back! Many of them had been placed in a minimum security facility in exchange for providing officials with information on other inmates. So they felt trapped and many simply took a walk. Out of fear, they began to escape from these minimum-security facilities. Several were taken back to the penitentiary and the pen began to go into a slow boil.

As Secretary, I would, from time to time, visit some of the facilities and talk to the staff and inmates. In September of 1979, a couple of inmates told me to get out of the system because something big was going to happen, and they did not want me to get caught up in what was to occur. They said that when the first snow fall occurred, that was when things were going to break loose. I passed this on to Felix Rodriguez and the warden. Felix came back and informed me that there was nothing to the warning., but they would keep an eye on things. A few weeks later, 11 of the most violent criminals in the penitentiary escaped. This was not the first snowfall, which leads me to believe that this was not an inmate-initiated action. There are various opinions as to how this happened or even why it happened.

On December 9, 1979, these 11 inmates escaped from the prison at Santa Fe. They left the prison, ran 50 yards across lighted areas in plain sight of the entrance tower, cut a hole in the interior fence and the concertina wire between the fences, then cut through the outer fence and ran to freedom. This prison escape raised many unanswered questions that the lawmakers, the media and the administration, for some strange reason, chose not to investigate.

The *Santa Fe New Mexican* ran an article on Thursday, March 19, 1981, as a result of the trial of William Norush, one of the prison escapees. Defense Attorney Robert Sera is quoted as saying, "Either a penitentiary officer set up the escape or the staff is so negligent and incompetent that it cannot be comprehended." "Earlier in the day," the article states, "inmate Leo McGill told the jury that before the escape he met with then Deputy Warden Robert Montoya, who wanted a major uprising in order to discredit his boss, Corrections Secretary Charles Becknell." After McGill made this statement, I received a call from the District Attorney, Eloy Martinez, who brought this to my attention. I asked Eloy if I could meet with this inmate to find out more. He said he would try to arrange it. When I heard from him again, McGill had been transferred to an out-of-state prison.

But, even before this, Senator Aubrey Dunn, at a hearing before the Senate Finance Committee, stated that he had heard that the inmates were let go to embarrass me and force me to resign. He asked me point blank if I had any knowledge about this. I told him I had no proof, but several employees had talked to me about the allegation. I was told that the female Corrections officers were told to call in sick and stay home that night. It was strange that on that night only a few Corrections officers were on duty (less than 30) to watch over 1,000 inmates. The word was apparently out; *something big is going down tonight.*

In the May/June 1980 edition of the *Rocky Mountain Magazine*, the writer states,

> Where are the wise men who, with their crystal balls, can look into the past and tell us why all this happened? The wise men are near the Plaza, in the heart of Santa Fe, in the Department of Criminal Justice, the Corrections Division. This is what they are saying:
>
> > The problem was the escape in December. It seems as if every-one knew about the escape beforehand except the warden and the top people. How else could eleven men get out? Perhaps the purpose was to get Charles Becknell, the Criminal Justice Department Secretary and the highest-ranking black official in New Mexico, to

> force him to resign. Though he was seeking higher pay for guards, he was also seeking higher standards; better performance. This was a threat to the guards and Becknell was vulnerable. Some people thought he was not doing his job well, and the redneck part of the Legislature had been trying to force him out for a year. And it worked; the uproar forced Becknell to resign. But the guards were the laughing-stocks because of it. They had to crack down inside. It happens after every escape. This new harassment of the inmates increased the tension until the men exploded.

One unanswered question that is puzzling is the length of time in which the escape took place. Harmon Ellis was an inmate escape artist from Arizona. He had escaped so many times in Arizona that prison officials shipped him to New Mexico. His last escape in Arizona had occurred while hiding in a couch that he knew was being removed from the prison. In New Mexico, he did not have to hide in a couch, overpower a guard or dig a tunnel. He just walked out. Harmon Ellis escaped several hours *after* the 10 men before him.

Accounts of his escape are so bizarre that one might find it unbelievable. He was in his cellblock, locked down for the night. Inmate after inmate came by and told him to come with them. They were getting out. He waited. Things just don't happen that way. He waited for the lights to come on, the sirens to go off or shots to be fired. Nothing happened. He walked outside and looked around for a hole in the fence. He circled the perimeter fence three times. He found the hole, looked around and waited for lights, guns, sirens, something. Finally, he said, "what the heck," and slipped off into the Santa Fe night. I don't recall how many hours had passed, but he went out long after the others.

Other unanswered questions are how did the inmates obtain the tools to cut the wire fence and how did they remove the barred window to enable their escape? What was the guard in the tower doing? Where were the officers who patrolled the perimeter of the Penitentiary? The report from the officer on duty that night, Captain Juan S. Romero, and other submitted reports, do not shed much light on the subject. The reports that were submitted read as follows:

Report #1:

The Penitentiary of New Mexico

Memorandum

To: Warden Griffin

From: Capt. Romero, Juan S. 1?C

Re: ESCAPEES Date Dec. 9, 1979

At approximately, 7:55 P.M. I had entered the Control Center, to get my 8:00 P.M. officeal count. I immediately received a call from my supervisors, who were patrolling the south side, Lt. Gonales, and Lt. Griego that a sheet, and jacket had been seen at the outside of the South Side Exit by the foot patrol, Officer Harrison. Also, the barbed wire, on the top of the cooridor roof, (south exit), the barbed wire, was cut and dropped to the ground

I, immediately prodeeded to the area, with the south exit key, went outside and found the area as reported to me. I, then proceeded to check the windows, of Cell Block #2, south side, and found the window bars cut, to cell #8. I then advised Capt. Martinez that there was an escape, and to advise all Towers, this was done, control center advised and the Deputy Warden called. I then secured, Cell Block #2, shut down all activities, and ordered a count of all living units. I went into Cell Block #2, after securing, and into cell #8, where I located one, dummy on the bed, one hack saw blade, and the big window pulled out forcibly, and the bars cut. The bars cut, were under the inmates bunk, not moved, left there for investigation.

I, proceeded to Cell Block #6 and secured that unit, at which time a count was being taken, and observed that some inmates were also missing from there. Capt. Martinez, was at the area and he continued the close observance of this unit, and reporting a total of 6 inmaes missing. No dummies found in this area and no cut bars.

All personel started reporting in after being advised of the incident. A count was reported, with a total of 11 inmates missing. Cell Block #2 had, 5 inmates missing and Cell Block #6 had 6 inmates unaccounted for.

All searches were initiated, per the superintendants orders, Mr. Koroneos, Inmates that were unaccounted for in Cell Block #2, are as follows:

Cell #8, Trujillo Jessie,#28322, Ellis, 26852 (corrected to 26815), Stevens, 26539, Stelly, #27110 (corrected to 27118) and Chapmen, #20064 (corrected to 28064)

Inmates that were unaccounted for in C.B.#6, are as follows:

Inmate # NoRush, 26832, Colby, 25651, Smith, 27215, Garcia, 24233, McGill, 25616, and Mascarenas, 28358.

All units remained secured and activities shut down.

Dist: Mr. Montoya

Mr. Koroneos

Mr. Morgan

Mr. Lujan

Mr. Rodriguez,

File.

(Copied exactly as report was submitted.)

Report #2:

The Penitentiary of New Mexico

MEMORANDUM

To: Capt. Romero

From: Urias, Lee H2 Officer

Re: Date

At approximately 810 Lt. B. Gonzales Lt. Griego – Officer Lee Urias were looking out the west window, South exit, Lt. Griego noticed the considine (corrected to contètina) wire from the roof on the ground in front of the west side window at South exit – Lt. Griego sp read the alarm w/ escape, at this time Lt. Gonzales reported to the control center, the incident; Advising Capt. Romero. Capt. Romero, immediately reported to the exit, with the key and went outside, found the wire on the ground, the jacket, and a sheet tied up in knots; like a ladder. He proceeded to the south of Cell Block #2 and reported one window cut, cell #8.

A shut down was ordered and a count was in process. Capt. Romero checked the cell and secured it. Inmate Trujillo, was assigned to this cell and was missing. A count was made and a total of five inmates were missing and accounted for.

Assigned inmates to this cell Block are 58 and only 53 were accounted for.

(Copied exactly as report was submitted.)

Report #3:

The Penitentiary of New Mexico

MEMORANDUM

To: Capt. Romero

From: Officer Hayes

Re: Date

At approximately 6:15 (corrected to 4:00 P.M.) I had been assigned to the north corridor patrol by Capt. Romero. I received a call at approximately 6:15 PM from Capt. Romero to go on foot patrol, inside the compound.

I proceeded to the control center and picked up the fence keys and stick and proceeded on the foot patrol. Tower #1 was advised of my being on foot patrol. Tower 1# advised me to check CB-6 exit area. I proceed to check and I found 1 sheet and it appeared to have been torn in two pieces. I continued on foot patrol, I then went around to the west area and checked all buildings and exits. I proceed in between CB-2 and f-1 dormitory clear up to the south exit. Returned towards the South area, D-1 Dormitory and around the east side of the penitentiary nothing unusual was noted by me on my patrol.

I was releived of my foot patrol duties by Officer Harrison. I returned to my official duties inside the institution.

(Copied exactly as report was submitted.)

Report #4:

The Penitentiary of New Mexico

MEMRANDUM

To: Capt. Romero

From: Officer James Harrison #174

Re: Date

At 7:20 PM I was relieved of duty in unit D-1 by Officer Hayes to go on foot patrol. I let tower #1 know I was going south to alert the other towers. On arriving between the south exit and cellblock #2 I discovered a cap, work jacket and a ladder made of sheets. I give these to Lt. Gonzales who was in the south corridor at the time. We also discovered that the wire had been pulled down from the top of the building in the same area. Lt. Gonzales immedely called Capt. Romero. Five more caps were found in the wire. I was joined by Cpat. Romero in checking the southside of cellblock #2 and the bars if cell #8 had been cut. Capt. Romero ordered me to the sally-port. I continued on partol.

(Copied exactly as report was submitted.)

Internal meetings with key staff regarding the incident revealed very little; I got a lot of vague responses. Prison staff reported to

Felix Rodriguez and he reported to the Governor, but I took the heat. There is a term that we hear among poker players, *know when to hold 'um and know when to fold 'um*. The time had come to *fold 'um*. I read an article that brought things back to reality. It was a community newspaper, I am not sure who the author was, but I saved it for some reason. Perhaps it was an encouragement to me at a time when I was getting stomped on pretty bad. The title of the article was "The Real Crime." It had as a caption "Notary Public: The Insider." The article is copied here as accurately as possible.

Notary Public: The Insider

The Real Crime

Watching our lawmakers at work and play provides some fascinating opportunities to study the elusive subject of logical thinking as it gets kicked around the corridors of the Roundhouse. One such recent treat occurred when on successive days the mugwumps of the Senate saw fit to shower accolades and embrazos on the latest felon to serve in that body, Emilio Naranjo, then diligently flayed the Secretary of Corrections for hiring to jobs other than janitorial, two men who have done time at the state pen.

With unbridled enthusiasm, the self-righteous spokesmen for public morality who emerge from the woodwork of the Senate chambers at the slightest provocation had a field day recently at the expense of Charles Becknell, head of the Department of Criminal Justice. With gusto, Mssrs. Schleintz, Dunn and similar backwoodsy types worked themselves into a froth of indignation over the imaginary sins that they were trying to pin on the record of one of the few capable King appointees and the only black man now serving in the cabinet.

To the mouth-agape amazement of the most hardened observers, Schleintz couldn't refrain from noting that of course his motives for the attack were free of racial taint, for his wife's "best friend is a black gal!" Senator Bilbo of Mississippi would have applauded such fervent open-mindedness.

As for Dunn, we've come to expect better. It has become customary for the press to heap praise on what passes for homespun wisdom and cracker-barrel economics in the burlesque environment of the Merry Roundhouse. Dunn, in particular, has come to be treated as some sort of reincarnation of Will Rogers, a latter-day apostle of common sense in government, a crafty legislative tactician , and a defender of bewildered New Mexican citizenry. In fact, however, as his finger-wagging treatment of Becknell clearly reveals, Dunn's attitude is more cracker than cracker barrel; his philosophy more Roy Rogers than Will Rogers, his use of power consistent with Fidel Castro's understanding of dissent.

This tendency toward thinking of himself as the guardian of all that is moral, right and inexpensive in our state sort of jumps out of Dunn at odd times, though it is generally kept under strict wraps. Last fall, though, it surged forth during hearings, on university budgets. Like some Charles Dickens character in search of an orphan or two to sneer at, Dunn embarrassed himself and his colleagues with a rambling, disjointed lecture on the, evils of the "Monty Python" television program. "Taxpayers' dollars spent on such frivolity," he mirthlessly intoned, "are a waste of money." It seems, you see, that the British humor show was being carried on the local PBS affiliate, KNME, which is under the responsibility of University of New Mexico. He demanded that such programming be removed.

Appropriating unto himself the role of flogger of sophomoric comedy is only the silliest of Dunn's excursions beyond his rightful-pale. For years, administrators of multimillion-dollar state programs have stoically endured red blistering at the Alamogordo legislator's hands over real or imagined peccadilloes committed by errant workers somewhere within their organizations.

Such scoldings only rarely surface in the media because he generally prefaces them with, "Now, this is off the record, but . . ." And woe be to any newsman or bureaucrat who would tempt fate by ignoring the chairman's request for silence on the matter.

I suppose such meddling in day-to-day administrative decision-making by a powerful legislator must be tolerated, however much violence it does to the notion of a tri-partite government - provided it remains within reasonable limits. Or at least, what recourse do we have? The good voters of Otero County (the same folks, incidentally, who bring you John Mershon of the House Appropriations and Finance Committee) see fit to continue inflicting him on the rest of us, so we can only suffer in silence, awaiting the relief that his eventual retirement will bring.

But occasionally his smug pomposity spills far beyond the bounds of reasonable behavior and demands some sort of response. Such is the case with his treatment of Becknell. Much eye-winking and rib-jabbing took place during that hearing, indications that the forces that were after Becknell's hide are confident that once the glare of the legislative spotlight is off, Gov. King will rush to rid himself of an administrator with the poor judgment to actually believe the sop his department puts out about rehabilitating criminals.

Although it does not seem too likely, King has the opportunity to act courageously and maintain his support of Becknell. After all, even Dunn shouldn't be allowed to blackmail the governor of New Mexico. We expect better than that of both of them.

Notary Public is the nom de plume of a strategically placed observer of the state and local political scene.

Attorney General Jeff Bingaman (now a United States Senator) was charged with the responsibility of investigating and writing a report on the escape incident. One day Jeff called me at my office and requested some information that he needed for the report. I asked if he was close to finishing the report. He said that he would be finished in about a week to 10 days. The next day, I saw Governor Bruce King, and he told me that he had had breakfast with Jeff Bingaman and that he had completed his work on the report and it was not favorable towards me. I had talked to Jeff the day before and he said that he was still working on the report. I called Jeff and asked him if he had misunderstood my question. He assured me that he was still working on the report. I asked him if he had had breakfast with the Governor and had they discussed the report. He said that he was at a breakfast with several people in attendance and he and the Governor had a brief conversation. "He asked how the report was coming and I told him that it was almost finished."

Time to fold 'um.

A couple of weeks prior to this, I had arrived at my apartment and saw this paper taped to my door. It was the straw that broke the camel's back. The heading was "Nigger Application for Employment." It read:

<u>NIGGER APPLICATION FOR EMPLOYMENT</u>

NAME______________________________ Date____________

Address____

(If living in automobile, give make, model, and license number)

Name of Mutha___________ Name of Fatha___________

Make of Automobile: Cadillac____________

Lincoln____________ Imperial___________

Number of Children Claimed on Relief_______

Number of Legitimate Children______________

Marital Status:

Common Law______________ Shacked Up_____________

Approximate Estimate of Income:

Theft$________Relief $_________ Unemployment______

Place of Birth: CharityHospital____FreePublicHospital___

Zoo________ BackAlley_________ Cotton Patch_______

How Many Words Can You Jive Per Minute?___________

Check Machines You Can Operate: Typewriter______ Adding Machine___ Telecopies____ Rubber Machine____

Check Foods You Like Best: BBQ______ Watermelon______Carp_______All of the Above_______

Check Illnesses You May Have Had in the Last Year: Measles_________Mumps__________

VD_____ Food Stamp Poisoning_____

Abilities: Government Employee_______

Demonstration Leader_______ Evangalist__________ Veneral Disease Spreader________ All of the Above_____

In 50 Words or Less, List Your Greatest Desire in Life: (Other than a White Person)

____

____

____

____, swears

(X or Signature)

that the info asked above is answered to the best of my nigger ability, and that I swears that I will always look like a nigger, act like a nigger, and smell like a nigger. I believes in the NAACP concept of equality, that niggers is better than white folks is. I promises to do everything in my power to increase the nigger population, so help me Lard! [typed as the original appeared]

The defining moment came when the Governor and I met at 7:30 on a Friday morning. The Legislature would be in session in a couple of weeks. He said that he felt I would still be an issue, and that would take the focus away from his legislative agenda and he did not want to fight this battle again. I asked him if it was time for us to part company. He felt that that would be a good idea. Governor King told me that he had a job lined up for me at the University of New Mexico and all I had to do was go and see Bud Davis, President of UNM, and he would get things arranged. After resigning, I made an appointment to see Bud Davis and he stated that he had no job for me. I was unemployed and left hanging out to dry. When you kick the system, the system will sometimes kick back with a vengeance, with the ultimate goal being total destruction. I was kicked by the best, but I survived. By the Grace of God, I survived!

Although the University of New Mexico has officially blackballed me to this present day, God has opened other avenues for me to survive. Survival is what it's all about. Survival with dignity is even better.

Chapter IX

The New Mexico Prison Riot

On February 3, 1980, I got an early morning call from a friend informing me that the inmates had taken over the prison and the institution was on fire. I said, "Oh my God!" There was too much information floating around for the prison officials not to be prepared for this. Meetings were held, information exchanged, reports were passed around – why was there no preparation for this? Was the Governor kept informed? I suspect not. I am puzzled as to why an investigative reporter did not follow-up on what practically everyone was talking about – something big is going to go down at the penitentiary. Historically, something big usually happened at the pen right before the legislative session anyway. Rumor has it that this was a tactic used by the penitentiary personnel for years in order to get the attention of the Legislature and to acquire additional funding.

On February 3, 1980, 33 human beings in the Santa Fe Prison died. The saddest part of this occurrence is that these 33 people died unnecessarily. They did not have to die! On that ill-fated, cold February night, posterity was abruptly terminated for 33 men. Some of these men were bludgeoned, some decapitated, and many others blow torched, maimed and burned to a slow torturous death.

For those who died, their legacies are marred by the fact that they lost their lives in one of the worse prison riots this country has ever experienced. Naturally, family members mourned their loss, but their deaths should be on the consciences of us all because the Santa Fe Prison riot *did not have to happen*! John Dunne once said, "No man is an island...Any man's death diminishes me." On February 2, 1980, in Santa Fe, New Mexico, society was diminished substantially because the blood that flowed in that prison, on that night, stains the hands and soulsof us all.

The riot of 1980 was not just an event that occurred; the riot was a result of policy direction becoming cloudy, misdirected and confused. The riot was the culmination of a failure to implement a planning process that had begun back in 1976, under the Apodaca era. Once a department does a 180-degree turn, within a short period of time, and without any alternative directions provided, chaos and confusion will surely follow.

In January of 1979, during the first few weeks of the King Administration, the Governor introduced a bill to effectively dismantle the Criminal Justice Department. The department was composed of a Criminal Support Division and the Administrative Services Division. Governor King's bill included the removal of the State Police Division from the Criminal Justice Department. The removal of the State Police Division alone would have had minimal effect on the function of the Department. However, the Legislature, acting on the wishes of the Governor, removed the Training and Education Bureau, which was the training function for the entire Criminal Justice system, including Corrections.

Once the Training and Education Bureau was removed from the Criminal Justice entity, it reverted back to strictly a law enforcement function. What was to happen to Corrections' training was not clearly defined since the Training and Education Bureau was now the Law Enforcement Academy. Most of the training staff remained with the Academy and others continued with the Corrections Department.

Corrections had no facility in which to train personnel; their roles were not clearly defined, and in essence, they had to start all over again. The training for Corrections officers was delayed at a critical point in the corrections planning process. With the removal of the State Police Department and the Law Enforcement Academy , the Criminal Justice Department became vulnerable, and even expendable.

Next came the Technical Services Bureau, which was placed under the State Police Department. The only bureau left under the Support Division was the Standards and Inspections Bureau. Then the Legislature awarded the Criminal Justice Support Division two additional divisions, Corrections and the Criminal Justice Support, which had zero appropriations. This left the Criminal Justice Department with two divisions – Corrections and Administrative Services; a dismantled department with a director who had no funding, and a Bureau dangling in the breeze with no place to go.

Then, the Legislature passed a law restricting the transfer of funds from one division to another. This move essentially killed the Criminal Justice Department, as it was known at that time. The Governor or the Legislature provided no future direction. Three years of planning came to a halt without an alternative plan being provided. At this point, the Criminal Justice Department was in shambles; morale was low, and with the removal of key Criminal Justice entities, the Department lost its identity and its focus. No one took the time to evaluate the devastating impact that dismantling the Department would have on the system of Corrections. Drastic shifts in policy direction, without planning or explanation, can cause confusion, and can impact negatively on improvements within the system.

After the Department was dismantled, the Corrections staff engaged in almost a total rebuilding program. The Department faced a situation where they were given a certain amount of money, a shell of a department, and told to go out and develop a model 20th century program. The Legislative Finance Committee was told quite specifically that *you can't expect to drive a Cadillac if you only have Chevrolet money.*

The demoralized staff began to rebuild the war-torn department and make personnel shifts within the budgetary restrictions of the new law. A staff retreat was held at D. H. Lawrence Ranch to establish new priorities and develop long-range plans.

Unfortunately, in November of 1979, the incident where several inmates at Camp Sierra Blanca Minimum Security Facility attacked and killed a fellow inmate had occurred. Five prisoners escaped, and were later recaptured. Some officials treated the incident as a sign that the whole Corrections system was falling apart, rather than what it actually was – a feud that had been brewing for a long time between several inmates. When these inmates got drunk and their courage was built up, a fight started and an inmate was killed. When you mix alcohol with bad feelings, the same situation can occur any place – in a person's home or in a local bar.

The Governor publicly called for a re-evaluation of all inmates at Camp Sierra Blanca, which would result in a return to the penitentiary for all inmates who were not "qualified" to be in a minimum security facility. The inmates became extremely uneasy. Some of them only had short terms, but they all felt that the worse thing that could happen to them at this point in their lives was to return to the "walls" (penitentiary). Some of the inmates simply walked away from Camp Sierra Blanca and the Los Lunas Honor Farm.

Inmates were transferred from Los Lunas for "re-classification," and 22 inmates were sent back to the penitentiary from Camp Sierra Blanca. This move contributed to the overcrowding problem at the pen, and inmate anger was aroused because some of them felt that they were being punished for something that they had no control over. By this time, the stage had been set for some type of retaliation from the inmates. Rumors began to flow frequently; the most persistent rumor was that inmates were going to take over the institution and conduct a mass escape.

After the Camp Sierra Blanca incident, as stated earlier, the Criminal Justice Department was being run by Felix Rodriguez as Division Director, Joanne Brown as Administrative Assistant, Bud Richards as the Chairman of the Corrections Commission, and Governor Bruce King. When the Penitentiary officials heard about the prison escape rumors, they dismissed them as having no basis. On December 9, 1979, the day before the Secretary's budget hearing before the Legislative Finance Committee, 11 of the most dangerous offenders at the State Penitentiary escaped unnoticed by prison officials.

Once the inmates were all returned, prison correctional officers who were embarrassed by the magnitude of the escape, and the backlash that followed, immediately began crack down procedures on the remaining inmates. Some prison officials were either fired or suspended by the Secretary of the Department, but some were reinstated or offered their jobs back at a later date.

As a result of overcrowding brought on partly by "re-classification," the crackdown by prison officials, mixed policy and directions, and the threat of inmate prosecution rumors once again began to flow regarding an event taking place that would be greater than the escapes.

After repeated racial attacks from some members of the Legislature, and after being sabotaged by some of my own staff members and some members of the Governor's staff, I resigned my position and the Corrections Department was without a leader. Three weeks later, on February 3, 1980, one of the worse prison riots known took place at the New Mexico State Penitentiary in Santa Fe.

The inmates took the total blame for the riot; however, administrative blunders played a greater role in bringing about this human tragedy that will never be forgotten.

When something of the magnitude of the prison riots of 1980 occur most people look for somewhere to place the blame. Real leadership required that someone take responsibility and say, *never again*! The horror of this prison riot was an experience like none we can imagine. Many questions about the manner of the deaths of the inmates were never answered; for instance, why was there such savage violence of inmate on inmate. The State Penitentiary officials had employed what was called a "snitch" system in which an inmate might pass on information about another inmate or give testimony during a trial. In return, a snitch could earn *good time*, be allowed to transfer to a minimum security facility or get a positive recommendation from prison officials when they appeared before the Parole Board. Some of the snitches were marked men when the riots began and revenge was taken on them in a brutal fashion.

Another tragedy of the riot was the unconfirmed rumor that not all of the slain inmates were accounted for. Thirty-three was the number that was given, but internal reports showed that there were inmates who could not be accounted for. The books were closed at 33 inmates, and that seemed to end the matter. The question still remains, were there others?

After the riots, and to this day, not one State official, reporter or Legislator has ever asked me about my insight into why the riot occurred. In 1982, to bring closure to my State government experience, I wrote a report on "What's Wrong with Corrections in New Mexico." Sadly, those issues are still relevant today. Can we have another prison riot? Yes, the ingredients for a riot are still very much a part of the system today.

Chapter X

More Politics

During the early part of 1986, I was asked by newly elected Mayor Ken Schultz to organize and direct the General Services Department for the City of Albuquerque. I was responsible for all of the City buildings and their maintenance, as well as vehicle maintenance, telephone services and energy management. I reported to Chief Administrative Officer Gene Romo. He was a good man who treated me fairly and gave me his full support.

After about a year on the job, Gene asked me to take over the position of Director of Personnel. I asked him, "Why me?" He responded, "The Mayor wants someone in the position who will run the department by the book. We are having too many problems, and he wants things cleaned up." I wanted assurances that I would not be forced to hire anyone who did not meet all of the requirements, and who did not go through the same process as everyone else. The Mayor agreed to this. I still believed that if someone gave their word, they meant what they said. I have been sold the Brooklyn Bridge many times, but overall, there are still many honest people in this world – even in the political arena. I enjoyed my job as Personnel Director. I had very little contact with the Mayor, and Gene Romo shielded me from a lot of interference from him (the Mayor). I did my best to keep politics out of the personnel process. Things were going quite well until Gene Romo was transferred to the Solid Waste Department and a new Chief Administrative Officer, Clarence Porky Lithgow, took over. The politics returned. Our relationship never developed into a good one because he did not adhere to the agreement of non-interference I had made with Gene. Many times I found myself saying *no* to Mr. Lithgow. Each time an employee says *no* to his/her boss, the relationship begins to deteriorate, and eventually, someone has to go. Usually it's the employee.

The Mayor lost his re-election bid, and he had about six weeks before he had to leave office. He wanted to move some people in his administration from exempt-appointed positions to classified positions; this was to protect them from removal by a new mayor. Lithgow came to my office with a list of eight names of people to be placed in classified or non-exempt positions. This was to be done without these people having to compete for the positions. I objected, and that was the final *no* answer that I would give my boss.

I asked Mr. Lithgow if he had discussed with the Mayor that this would be a violation of the City's Merit Ordinance. His response to me was, "The Mayor wants this done." I asked if I could speak to the Mayor about this issue and Lithgow told me, "The only thing that the Mayor wants to hear is that it's done." I offered to put together the paperwork and he or the Mayor could sign to make the transition from exempt to non-exempt. Lithgow said, "We want you to sign." I told him that I could not do it.

At that moment, I felt that my days were numbered; I had refused an order from my boss. I was standing in the way and I had to be removed. Lithgow informed me that "if you won't do it, we will find someone who will." The line had been drawn in the sand. I made the decision to hold my ground. Some issue was needed to remove me from my position, and I had inadvertently handed it to them.

A sitting City Councilor made a request for address labels for all of the City employees. He was also a candidate for the Office of Mayor. We had some boxes of unused address labels that had been in the office for weeks. I gave those to the Councilor. He did his political mailings to City employees, and things got ugly after that. The complaints came pouring in that someone had provided a political candidate a mailing list of City employees. The Mayor spoke out, then the press got involved, and the witch-hunt was on.

Things began to spin out of control; the press smelled blood. While the search was on for the culprit, I began to ask myself the questions, *What do I do about this dilemma*? *Do I come forward or do I hide out*? No one would ever know, and I could go on, wait out the Mayor, and on a good news day the media would go on to something else. But I had been raised to never live a lie. When I went to Lithgow and told him the truth I knew that I had a lot to lose, but I also knew that it was the right thing to do.

Shortly thereafter, Lithgow came to my office with a yellow writing tablet. He placed it in front of me and said, "The Mayor wants your resignation." I refused and asked him why couldn't they wait until they had received the results of the investigation they had initiated. He placed me on administrative leave, and I was told to clean out my desk and go home. A few days later, I received a certified letter advising me of my termination.

The results of investigations by both the City and the District Attorney concluded that there was no wrongdoing on my part. However, by this time I had been demonized, and the press had a field day. Channel 4 sent a reporter with a camera to my house even though I had already told TV anchor Tom Joles that I did not want to speak to anyone. The cameraman rang my doorbell and filmed my wife when she came to the door. When the report was issued to the City from their own investigator no one wrote a story, printed the truth or even stated that there was no wrongdoing on my part. I requested a copy of the report, but I was refused. The choice I had made to be fired rather than to resign was based on principle.

During my short time with the City of Albuquerque I saw employees on all levels abuse the system. I witnessed fraud, drunk driving, spousal abuse, theft and numerous other offenses -all that the abusers received was a slap on the wrist. My expectation was to be treated fairly. I expected some penalty for my error in judgment, but I was not prepared for the political and racial reaction that prompted what felt like the *death penalty*.

Experience has shown me that usually when a white person breaks a rule it is considered a misdemeanor, but a black person will receive the *death penalty* for the same offense. Whether we want to admit it or not, there are still double standards in our society today.

I had no recourse because I was an "at will" employee, serving at the pleasure of the mayor. I filed a charge with the Equal Employment Opportunity Commission (EEOC), but I found out that the principal investigator had gone to high school with Lithgow. EEOC issued a "no probable cause" ruling on the claim of racial discrimination. Case closed!

The firing from the City of Albuquerque Personnel Department has hurt my pursuit of other employment opportunities, but given the choice I would make the same decision today. Standing on principle may not put food on the table, but it sure makes for a good night's sleep.

Chapter XI

Looking Back

Satchel Page once said, "Don't look back, something might be gaining on you." In the Bible, Lot's wife was told not to look back, but she did and turned into a pillar of salt. If one dwells in the past, he/she will not be able to see the future. A person cannot look backward and forward at the same time. Dwelling in the past does not leave any room for forgiveness. When I received that call from Senator Ken Schleintz's wife informing me that he had passed away but wanted her to find me and ask for my forgiveness, I went into prayer and forgave all those who had brought pain into my life. Instead of looking back, I had to look to God; He was all I had and all I that I have now.

I could imagine how Job felt when his friend told him that he must have done something wrong because he was going through so many trials and tribulations. Many of my friends were not sure; they felt that I had to do something to bring this kind of reaction from those in power – these attacks were too vicious to be unmerited. I have learned from my years of experience in the political and spiritual arenas that in order to crucify, you must first vilify. This gives justification to the crucifixion process. That year I served in the King administration was the most traumatic year of my life. What amazes me is that no one checked the tremendous progress we had made in Corrections. No one looked at the way we addressed the issues and how we solved the day-to-day problems. No one looked at how I put together a staff that worked as a team, looking at long-term solutions to problems that had been accumulating over the years.

Besides the issue of race, one of the main focuses of the attacks seemed to be aimed at two employees who had past criminal records. Both men had done their time, received pardons and were productive and trustworthy members of the department. My God, what is rehabilitation all about? How long does a person have to pay? Shouldn't we forgive and bring them back into the mainstream of our society? If we don't afford ex-convicts the opportunities to make a living, but keep punishing them for something they have already served time for, guess where they are going to end up? Back in our institutions at $25,000 to $35,000 a year, at our expense! It seemed more realistic to me to allow them to work in a $20,000 to $30,000 a year job and pay taxes. The point that many fail to grasp is that at some point an inmate will come out. Unless serving a sentence without possibility of parole or on death row, he or she *will come out and return to our communities*! Do you want a person who is worse than he was when he went in or one who has been rehabilitated? The Corrections Department has always been caught in a catch-22 situation. Recidivism has continually been a big issue. Inmates keep on coming and going through that revolving door. If nothing is done to alter this situation, the problem will continue to grow, the finger pointing will intensify and blame will be thrown around like a football. Someone once said, if you change nothing, nothing will change. The misguided perception is that if an inmate sits locked up for the duration of his sentence, at the end he will walk away a changed man. He will learn his lesson and now be a productive member of society.

I believed in treating inmates with respect because when you take away a man's dignity, you have created an enemy. A man with no dignity left becomes a security risk and a threat to the lives and well being of other inmates and correctional officers. It is easy for people who don't see inmates every day or come in contact with them to refer to these people as "animals" and demand that they be treated as such. But every time a person in a suit imposes harsh sanctions on inmates, the corrections officer is the one who suffers the consequences.

Some people were making decisions about Corrections who had never even been to a correction institution. They had this image of inmates as mad, out of control, hard-core rapists and murderers who needed to be locked up forever. They overlooked the fact that many of these people have families, as well as their communities, to which they do return. I strongly supported the concept of sending inmates back into their communities as better fathers, husbands, sons, daughters, sisters, brothers and citizens. For this philosophy, I was called a liberal and punished. Liberal is a term I embrace and I wear it proudly. However, contradictions came into play when it came to managing the budget for the department; then I was called conservative. I wore that label proudly also. My attackers never discussed my accomplishments in Corrections, or what plans were on the drawing board. What some labeled as *liberalism*, I called *vision.*

When I took over as Secretary of Corrections, Mike Hanrahan was head of the Department of Corrections. He hired Lloyd McClendon as one of his top assistants. Lloyd McClendon had served a term in the State Penitentiary on a murder conviction. I don't remember the kind of reaction being shown to Hanrahan when he hired a murderer that I received for hiring an embezzler or a safecracker. Why? Double standards? Politics or race? Perhaps we will never know.

Part of the problem with Corrections was a lack of continuity in leadership. Since Felix Rodriguez had served as Warden,

Corrections had changed wardens and secretaries so often that it was almost impossible to bring about stability in the system. The classified staff knew that when a new Governor came in, the appointed leadership would change. At some point, the tail wags the dog. I was appointed Secretary of the Criminal Justice Department by Governor Apodaca and confirmed by the Senate with little or no opposition. I served as Secretary for two years under Apodaca and no one questioned my competency. Under Bruce King, overnight I became incompetent! I have never been one to quickly play the race card, but when you have five cards in your hand and they all say "race," those are the only cards you can play.

Corrections was one of Governor Apodaca's priorities during his administration. He gave the Department the support it needed and recognized the fact that Corrections had a long way to go. Unfortunately, Corrections had to compete for scarce resources with education, social services, health care and other programs. However, the amount of resources made available during Jerry Apodaca's administration increased significantly. Although not enough to make up for years of neglect, the amount received showed that Governor Apodaca gave Corrections strong, vocal and consistent support.

Shortly after I was appointed, Governor Apodaca requested a comprehensive study be prepared to look at the State's Corrections system. He wanted us to develop a long-range plan that would provide focus and direction for years to come. As a result, a series of comprehensive bills were presented in the 1977 and 1978 legislative sessions designed to deal with immediate and long-term problems. Not every proposal was accepted, but the record was quite impressive. Two new facilities were authorized, a medium security facility at Los Lunas and another facility near Roswell. The Honor Farm at Los Lunas was renovated and expanded. Existing statutes were amended to authorize and operate an intake and classification center. Although the request for appropriation of a separate facility to house the center was denied, approval of the concept was a significant first step in upgrading the State's correctional system.

My intent was to take what we could get and come back later for the rest. Properly implemented, the intake and classification center would be responsible for (a) developing a complete history on each inmate, and (b) assigning the inmate to the appropriate institution based on the level of security he or she needed. Staff could then monitor each inmate periodically to review and make recommendations on classification levels. This allowed for the efficient use of all institutions, consequently, relieving pressure on the penitentiary.

One of my big concerns was the lack of training for Corrections personnel. I wanted to tie training to an upgrade in pay for the officers. Most of all, I saw training as an investment. Unfortunately, the decision made in the Legislature saw funding for training merely as an expenditure. Training would also be used as a means of upward mobility, as well as better pay. Consequently, as part of Governor Apodaca's reorganization package, the Law Enforcement Academy was merged into the Criminal Justice Department and became the Bureau of Training and Education.

Prior to this time, the Law Enforcement Academy had been used exclusively for law enforcement training, and for several days of the month it remained idle. There were no dedicated facilities for training Corrections personnel, so it made sense to use the Academy for this purpose when the police were not using it. When we began to use the Academy for Corrections' training, the cops went into orbit. This was no longer their facility; it now came under the Bureau of Training and was being utilized by all department employees for training functions. The State Police still had priority, but not exclusive control. When Governor King came into office, this was one of the first functions of the department to be dismantled. The State Police got their facility back and no longer had to report to "Leroy."

In spite of what was viewed and reported, with only assumptions based on external factors, there was a great deal of progress made in Corrections during my tenure. Some of those included:

- Planning and opening of the Roswell Correctional Center.
- Planning and opening of the Radium Springs Center for Women.
- Reduction of the State Penitentiary inmate population from 1,300 to less than 1,000.
- Creation of the Corrections Education Department with central administration for all education programs.
- Legislative approval for placing Corrections Education Programs on the State's public schools funding plan.
- Implementation of a new semi-protection unit at the State Penitentiary.
- Opening of a new residential lodge at the Boys School.
- Planning and implementation of the first joint Judicial Corrections State seminar.
- Capital outlay planning fund for a new recreation center and school at the Youth Diagnostic Center.

- Upgrading of job classifications for adult parole officers, juvenile correctional officers and adult correctional officers.
- Establishment of a culinary arts program for women at the State Penitentiary.
- Legislative approval of the following:
    - Intake and Classification Center
    - Juvenile re-integration program
    - Expansion of mobile forensic teams
    - On-line computer system
- Creation of a women's inmate section and appointment of women's section chief.
- Creation and appointment of the Minimum Security Classification Committee and development of minimum security transfer criteria.
- Creation of the Safety and Health Standards Division.
- Creation of a Juvenile Institution Program Evaluation Committee.
- Development of the Northern New Mexico College vocational program for the Penitentiary.
- Creation of the Standards and Inspection Bureau.
- Creation of a Juvenile Detention Fund ($4 million)
- Delancey Street Drug Treatment Program brought to the State of New Mexico

When we look at the amount of monetary resources made available to Corrections between 1975 and 1978, the record reflects significant increases in response to aggressive efforts by the Apodaca administration. But, unfortunately, we were playing catch-up and there were no pat answers to years of neglect. Corrections needed, and still needs, a sustained financial commitment. As long as people are being sent to prison, Corrections needs to have a strong commitment from the Governor and the Legislature. Otherwise, the neglect will catch up with us again.

Sure, mistakes were made, but they were honest mistakes and not made due to a lack of trying. In my mind, the vision was clear. Translating that vision to the Legislature was quite difficult, but some of the legislators understood and gave strong support. However, there was enough blame to go around. At that time, blame placing was the order of the day. I believe, however, that to whine because of false accusations weakens your resolve. As Governor Jerry Apodaca used to say, "No excuses, just results."

Perhaps one of the reasons Jerry and I are such good friends today is because we share a common experience. We have both been falsely accused, beaten up by the media and our reputations have been tarnished. But probably more importantly, we both believe that there is a God and He will straighten things out in

His own time and in His own way. Because of the publicity surrounding my firing by Governor King, no one would hire me. I had a family to take care of, bills to pay and I was about to exhaust my savings, having already withdrawn monies from my retirement fund. My faith was all that kept me going. I had a lot of questions. One of my big questions was why had the media come after me with such force? I came to realize that other people see us differently than we see ourselves and when you kick the system, especially if you are black, the system will kick back and teach you a lesson. If you are black and you live in New Mexico, if the police can't get to you, the media will. Then your place of employment gets involved, and the result is unemployment, ostracism or both.

Most of the reporters that I encountered were friendly and some I could actually call "friend." I asked one reporter why the *Albuquerque Journal* usually slammed me. The response was, "Don't take it personal. It's not about you, it's about the story. You are a story." I asked him, "What about the truth?" He replied, "As long as it's not a lie, we are within the boundary lines." Wow! One can take the truth and make it look different, and regardless of the harm it does, it's okay. I still wrestle with that explanation.

Fred McCaffrey was one of my favorite reporters. I respected his honesty, his integrity and his genuine concern for humanity. Fred wrote the first article ever written on my activities. He was a rare breed in the field of journalism because he really cared about people. This was reflected in his reporting. Bill Feather and Larry Calloway were fair, decent and honorable men. The stories they wrote had a balance that reflected fairness. I respected David Steinberg a great deal. I came to realize that stories written for the print media go to an editor and this is where stories are chopped up and rearranged. David was a real trooper.

In the electronic media, except for Jane Metzgar, I have little respect for any of the television anchors with whom I came in contact. Tom Dunn of KOB radio was a friend and I truly regretted his passing. Integrity is something that cannot be bought, sold, traded or bestowed on a person. It comes from within. The people mentioned above exuded integrity.

My relationship with the media reflects what many African Americans already knew - there are different standards for blacks and for non-blacks. I was naïve enough to believe that by earning a Ph.D., I would be treated like everyone else with the same degree. I believed that it carried the same value for blacks as it did for whites. I was also naïve enough to believe that by being a Cabinet Secretary, I would be treated like other Cabinet

Secretaries. I had *earned* my place at the table, just like the others. The dual standard was reflected in how I was treated. I was in a place where, in the minds of society, I had no right to be. I stood out and therefore became fair game. In a sense, I had kicked the system. I was in a place reserved for someone else of a different color. Just by my being there, being at the table and being black, the system kicked back. But thank God, he gave me the strength to keep getting up. If one does not get up, there will be the tendency to give up.

With all that had taken place, I can still say that I am a Democrat – a lifelong, liberal Democrat. Ever since I can remember, my step-father has been involved in Democratic Party politics. Candidates for office would stop by our house soliciting his support. During the campaign season, I can remember signs and banners all over our yard, and on my step-dad's car and pick-up truck. Over the years, he became very influential in Lea County politics. He was one of the individuals that Democrats knew they needed if they were going to be successful. During the early years of my life, the candidates for office were exclusively white. We would see them during election time, and usually did not see them again until the next election. My step-dad knew them all and they all knew him.

When I turned 21, while I was still in college, I registered to vote and became a registered Democrat. I have worked in the Democratic Party for years. I served as Chairman of the Affirmative Action Committee when Ben Alexander was State Chairman. I find it ironic that practically every time I have been attacked and harmed by politicians it has been by a fellow Democrat! Most of the meanness and viciousness I have experienced in the political arena has come not from Republicans, but from Democrats.

Although I am not as active in party politics as I once was, I don't believe in party switching. I believe that to go to bed as a Democrat and wake up a Republican, or vice versa, is to wake up a turncoat. So I have remained a Democrat, but not one who is as committed as I once was. When all is said and done, it’s not the party affiliation or the color of the skin that counts; it's what's in a person's heart.

In the spring of 1980, I was becoming nervous about my financial condition and I started to think about seeking employment out of state. Then I heard about a position at the Gas Company of New Mexico's Corporate Office. This information came to me by what some would classify as an accident, but when God is involved, there are no *accidents*. He has a purpose for us all. I decided to apply. When I did, another man had just been hired. A couple of days later, I received a call and was informed that the man they hired had a medical situation and could not report to work. I was asked, "Are you still available?" I tried to contain my excitement. I interviewed for the position and was hired. After several weeks of being unemployed and virtually *blackballed* (excuse the pun) in State government and the University, I finally had my dignity restored.

I reported directly to the President, Bill Barnhouse. Bill was exactly what I needed at the time. He was a great boss and a kind Christian man. Above all, Bill was supportive and he was fair. The home office, Southern Union Gas, gave him a lot of flack about wanting to hire me, but Bill stood his ground.

As part of the hiring process, corporate executives had to be interviewed by a company psychiatrist in Dallas, Texas. I flew to Dallas and went to my appointment. About an hour into the conversation, I ended up counseling the interviewer on problems he was having with his kids. We had a role reversal; he ended up on the couch, so to speak, and I began to question him and give advice. At the end of two hours, he felt better, but I wasn't sure what had happened to me. When I returned to the office in Albuquerque, Bill asked me how things had gone. I told him what happened and he got a big laugh from my report.

God usually sends people into your life to fulfill a need you have at that time. Bill Barnhouse and I became good friends and we remain friends to this day. His first wife, Margaret, was a remarkable woman and a great friend also. She has gone on to be with the Lord, but I still miss her cheerful conversation, her words of encouragement, and her black-eyed peas on New Year's Day. If every parent in America raised their children the way Bill and Margaret did, there would be no racial problems in America and race would be a non-issue.

After three months on the job at the Gas Company, Bill told the Secretary to tell me to come to his office. He wanted to talk to me about my expense report. I entered his office and sat down. I thought to myself, *Becknell, you have only been here three months and you have screwed up already*. Bill reminded me that I was responsible for community relations and my expense reports were so small that it did not reflect community involvement. My first report was around $40 for the entire month. Most of that was gasoline for the company car.

I had never been in the corporate world before; my work experience had always been in the public sector. We had no expense accounts in public service. As a public servant, I would not allow someone else to buy my lunch or dinner. I either paid for my own or I picked up the entire tab. I had carried this practice over into the private sector. I told Bill that I was paying out of my own pocket when I took people to lunch or dinner. He explained to me how the system worked in the private sector, but old habits die hard.

I have been blessed to have some great bosses throughout my career and I learned from each. From my first principal Dever Langhoff, I learned professionalism and to think things through before acting. It took some time for that to sink in. He was a good role model for anyone desiring to rise to a higher level of professionalism. From the Vice President of the University of New Mexico, Chester Travelstead, who also was my supervisor, I learned patience and how to treat people with dignity. You don't have to yell, scream and belittle to get someone's attention. From Jerry Apodaca, I learned about courage and standing up for what you believe in, even if it is unpopular. I was in Jerry's presence when he made some unpopular decisions as Governor, but he would always say, "It's the right thing to do." I admired Jerry because he was no hypocrite. And from Bill Barnhouse at the Gas Company, I learned that you can be humble, yet strong. I also learned compassion. All of these outstanding men touched my life in many other ways, and I will be eternally grateful to them all.

In 1980, while still working at the Gas Company, I came to realize that I am a teacher. I believe God gave me this talent, and the call to teach grew stronger and stronger. After leaving the Gas Company, and still unable to obtain re-employment at UNM, I decided to start my own company, oriented towards training and human development. I opened my doors as Becknell and Associates. The going was rough at first, but I made the decision to work hard, trust God, treat my customers fairly, and exhibit a high degree of professionalism.

I discovered early on that if I was going to be successful, I had to seek business outside of the State of New Mexico. There were two factors that influenced this decision. The first was related to race. Companies at that time would not even entertain the idea of allowing me to present a workshop to their employees. This concept was new to most companies. They were used to seeing white trainers, and this was the image they were willing to pay for. I knew it would take time to change these attitudes, but I did not have that kind of time. I had a family to support and I had to bring in an income.

As a consultant, my business adventures have included trips to many cities in the United States, as well as Puerto Rico, the U.S. Virgin Islands, the Bahamas and Liberia, West Africa. I have trained managers and supervisors at IBM, AT&T and many federal, state, city and county agencies. I am most proud of the fact that most of my business has been repeat clients. Praise be to God from whom all blessings flow!

The second factor that drove me to seek business outside of the State of New Mexico was the seemingly unfair competition coming from University professors. These trainers were able to charge a lower fee for their services because they were already on salary at the University of New Mexico; so their involvement in the training profession was secondary income. They had University resources, such as secretaries, to do their typing (paid for by the University), telephones, offices and research, paid for by the University, as well. Essentially, they had no overhead. Consequently, they could charge less. Their involvement in the training profession was to finance a trip to Europe during the summer; mine was to put food on the table.

God has blessed me and provided opportunities for me to generate an income. Racism has at times interfered with my business pursuits. Once, as an 8(a) contractor, I obtained a sizeable contract from a federal agency. To finalize the contract, I had to obtain a signature from the local Small Business Administration (SBA) office. This office was required to assist me to meet all the requirements of the contract. When I presented this contract opportunity to them, instead of helping me, they responded by initiating an investigation to find out how I got the contract in the first place. In spite of the SBA, I was still able to obtain the contract and perform the necessary requirements.

Chapter XII

Where Do We Go From Here?

Frederick Douglass, the great black abolitionist once said, "Power concedes nothing without a demand." If we don't challenge racism, we will not make this a better place for future generations. *No challenge, no change*! I am convinced that nothing will change as long as the victim has the responsibility for the eradication of the problem. This situation has and will continue to place the victim in the position of either begging or being perceived as always complaining. Either way, the perception that the victim of racism is a problem, and has to be punished or ignored, needs to be changed.

Racism is not always visible and for those who have never been affected by racism, it is not always identifiable. Consequently, it becomes difficult for some to comprehend what victims of racism are talking about when they say, "I have been discriminated against." The response from the person that has not known what discrimination is or how it feels will often be "You're overreacting or I don't see it."

Sometimes the persons who state that they have been discriminated against can't describe it themselves, but they *feel* it. They have experienced that feeling before and they know what discrimination feels like. I have found that it is difficult to describe to someone what it feels like to be discriminated against when they have never had that experience. I have often read articles and heard statements and commentaries made by people who don't have a clue as to what the victim feels or how the victim is affected. The problem of racism will not be solved until all people come together and form a common agenda.

I heard a lecture once, and the speaker made a pretty profound statement about race relations. He stated, "A large number of white people in our society do not know more than five black people; most don't know any." He differentiated between *know* and *acquainted.* To *know* is to have information about that person's family, culture, likes and dislikes; to share a meal together and share intimate thoughts. To be *acquainted* is to recognize that person and say *hello* and *goodbye.*

People who don't *know* African Americans are making decisions about our lives, our employment and futures on jobs and in the classrooms without consulting us. Quite often, decisions are made on assumptions rather than facts.

Currently, we live in a society where there are dual standards. When we have one set of standards or one set of rules that apply equally to all, and when black people are afforded the same rights and privileges as white people, then we will be on our way to eradicating racism in our lifetime.

Another reason that racism may be hard to identify is that it can wear many masks. I have encountered many, if not all, the masks of racism that can be worn. In 1964, I was a senior at the College of St. Joseph (University of Albuquerque), a Catholic institution. There were probably no more than a dozen African American students on campus; only three or four of those were female. Consequently, some of the African American males were dating white and Hispanic females. Some of these female students revealed that one of the nuns at the college had called their parents and told them that their daughters were dating African Americans. Some of the parents gave their daughters a stern warning about the consequences involved in dating outside their race. Two parents drove to Albuquerque, loaded up their daughters and pulled them out of school, never to be seen again.

I was confused because Christians were not supposed to be that way. Acts of racism are contrary to what the Bible teaches. My first reaction was to boycott the next basketball game by refusing to play. That would show them! I calmed down and decided to go see Father Morrison, a priest and professor on campus. He was a friend to all students and a man I respected. He understood my anger and confusion, and he told me that before I made the decision to refuse to play the next game to listen to what he had to say. He told me, "Charles, there are three kinds of people in this world. There are good people, bad people and very nice people. You know where the good people stand, and you know where the bad people stand. It's the very nice people that you have to watch out for." From that point on, I became leery of the *very nice people*. A few of the nuns were *very nice people*.

My journey through the maze of racism in New Mexico has taught me many lessons. Among those, good people in certain circumstances can turn into *very nice people* or bad people. Bad people can turn into good people. But the *very nice people* are the most dangerous of the three because they are always going to be the *very nice people.* They fool you with a smile, confuse you with words that contradict who they are, and they mislead you with a handshake and a pat on the back. I have been done in by a lot of *very nice people*. The masks worn can be religious, as well as individual or political.

To be black and live in New Mexico is to face obstacles that are difficult to overcome because most of the obstacles are based on race, rather than competence. In many cases, preparation and education do not open the door to opportunity for African Americans in New Mexico. I have asserted on numerous occasions that in New Mexico, there is a definite pecking order in terms of employment and services. In most cases, after the Anglo, the Hispanic and the Native American, there is not much left for blacks.

Black males are rapidly becoming an endangered species in New Mexico, falling victim to unfair stereotypes and being incarcerated in our prison system at percentages that are almost three times the size of our population. The school dropout rate for African Americans in Albuquerque is about four out of ten kids. In a 1995 article in *Emerge* magazine, I was shocked when I read:

> "From cradle to grave, Black males languish at the bottom of virtually every societal measure of well-being, from infant mortality to life expectancy. Black baby boys die before their first birthday at a rate that is more than twice that of White baby boys. The gap between Black and White infant mortality has widened since the 1970s, with Black babies dying at twice the rate of Whites. At the other end of life, while White Americans live an average six years longer than

> African Americans, the 66-year life expectancy of Black males is seven years shorter than White males, nearly nine years shorter than Black females and almost 14 years less than the 79 years White females can expect."

A few years ago, I conducted a workshop for the U.S. Department of Agriculture for approximately 25 black male employees. These men had attained grade levels close to the top of the pay scale and the next step would be the position of Senior Executive Service. They were frustrated because the opportunities for creative assignments and advancement were now passing them by. They had become victims of Affirmative Action because they felt pushed aside and now the emphasis was being placed on women and other minorities. They expressed that they were the ones who had fought the battles, paid the price and opened the doors, but now they were being passed over.

These were examples of black men who had bought into the system. They had gone to many of the predominately black schools, and they cameinto the workplace with strong family and religious values. They had done all the right things. They attended workshops and seminars and had followed all the rules. Not only were they competent, they were at the *top of their game*, so to speak. Now they were being passed by, and they were confused, hurt and angry.

When they questioned or brought up concerns, the typical response was, "What are you complaining about? You make a good salary." Or "Aren't you happy here? There are other places that you can work. You are lucky you have a job." If they questioned things or even asked questions they were labeled as troublemakers, and their careers were placed on hold. Many of the men in that room were in that category and they were angry, bewildered and demoralized. They tried to use humor to maintain their sanity. I heard statements like,

"What do you call a black man who has a job?"

"Lucky!"

"What do you call a brother on vacation?"

"Happy!"

"What do you call a brother who is retired?"

"A free man!"

"What does he say on his last day before retirement, as he walks through the door?"

"Free at last, free at last, thank God Almighty, I'm free at last!"

I am sure that white people would say the same thing but with a different meaning.

So these men learned to cope by hiding. They stopped making suggestions because they did not want to appear as though they were challenging the system. They learned to dress down so that they did not look too important and did not dress better than their white bosses. One of the participants told me that every two years he bought a new car, but he drove a second car to work that was an older model. He felt that if his boss saw him in a new car, and it was better than the car his boss drove, the assumption would be made that he was doing fine and did not need a promotion or a raise. They had learned what it took to survive in the workplace.

These black men had come into the workforce, prepared themselves and worked hard. They had made numerous significant contributions to their agencies and tried to apply the skills and knowledge that they had acquired only to hit a brick wall. They saw the good old boy network working 24-7. They watched in quiet humiliation and stood on the sidelines as others became the beneficiaries of the opportunities that they had fought so hard to attain. Perhaps the greatest humiliation comes when these black men and others in the workplace today learn to hide by leaving a part of themselves at the gate before they enter their places of employment.

As African Americans, we have to live in two different worlds, one black and one white. Each world makes demands on us, but we learn to live with double standards and the pecking order of privilege. Whites deny that they have privilege, but on the other hand they protect whatever it is that they deny that they have.

While growing up in Hobbs we learned that white policemen were to be feared; we also knew that they were there to protect and serve the interest of the white community. Their job was to preserve white privilege. We were all taught our *place*, so privileged and underprivileged was ingrained in all of us at an early age. Many will deny this, but most will accept privilege when it is extended. Affirmative action and selective hiring has always been a part of the white power structure.

Laws and covenants have been established to preserve white privilege. A few short years ago, admission to law schools and medical schools was reserved for the privileged. This was an affirmative action program that was based on a quota system that no one from the white community complained about. The admission of blacks and other minorities into these schools interfered with white privilege. Therefore, a great deal of protest has come from the white community. The protest against Affirmative Action is not about equality – Affirmative Action interferes with white privilege.

When Rosa Parks refused to move to the back of the bus, she interfered with white privilege. White privilege assumes that when a black person is hired or promoted that it is because of Affirmative Action, rather than competence. When a black person is next in line and the service person ignores him/her and helps the white person who is second in line, white privilege is being assumed. If the white person does not say anything, this is *accepting* white privilege.

The battle for challenging racism cannot rest solely in the hands of black people. White people must speak up as well. The issue of privilege is one that the *privileged* will have to confront and decide whether to refuse, until the same privilege is extended to all. For most, this will be difficult to do because along with privilege comes comfort. To sacrifice one's position can bring about a great deal of discomfort.

We delude ourselves and live under the illusion of a colorblind society; one where hiring and upward mobility are not based on race. This illusion denies the existence of privilege. There is a tendency to deny that the same choices and opportunities are not available to all.

It is my personal opinion that racism is a form of violence. Racism can destroy a person's self-esteem and self-image. When a man is denied an opportunity for a job because of his race, this has a devastating impact on his entire family. This is equivalent to taking food off his table; thus, he can't feed his family. The family then goes into a crisis situation. Employment discrimination based solely on race should fall under the category of a hate crime. One would really have to hate another person to deny him the opportunity to eat. This may seem harsh, but I offer no apology.

The atmosphere for African Americans in New Mexico is not one of hostility, but one of indifference. This may not be true on an individual basis or in one's close circle of friends, but overall, I feel this statement to be true.

In order for racism to be diminished in New Mexico and for African Americans to be given an opportunity to be a part of the cultural mosaic, the following initiatives need to occur:

- **Become more inclusive.** From the highest to the lowest level, all citizens need to refrain from referring to New Mexico as a tri-cultural state. To exclude is to ignore and to devalue. We need to create a more positive atmosphere regarding African Americans by saying, "You are also important." Most of all, "You belong and we welcome you to the table."

- **Teach African American History.** Teach units of African American history in all of the public schools in New Mexico. Emphasis should be placed on the history of the contributions African Americans have made to the State of New Mexico, and to America in general. This would bring about a greater appreciation of African Americans.

- **Churches need to get involved.** Churches should initiate dialogues on race relations and develop programs to change attitudes toward African Americans. Churches should speak out on injustices and inequities. To do less is hypocritical. When the dignity of one is lessened, we all lose. Many church people work in government positions, sit on corporate boards, are in classrooms and other levels of our society. If they begin to challenge, things would change.

- **Increase employment opportunities.** Government entities, state, county, city and municipal agencies need to do a spot assessment. If they have no African Americans employed in any capacity, they need to move affirmatively to train and employ qualified African Americans. The same holds true with the private sector. For instance, when I enter a bank, I look around to see if that bank employs people who look like me. We, as African Americans, bank at banks that won't hire us, buy cars from dealerships that won't even interview us, and pay taxes to fund government agencies that won't extend services or employment opportunities to us.

- **Invest in black businesses.** Government agencies and private businesses should actively seek out black businesses and extend contracts to them so that these businesses can grow and hire other African Americans. Also, banks should make it easier for African American businesses to acquire low-interest loans to expand their businesses. The Small Business Administration needs to change its attitude toward African American businesses and provide services on an equitable basis.

- **Support self-help organizations**. Organizations like the NAACP, The National Council of Negro Women and other local organizations are designed to help improve conditions for African Americans. They are not designed to destroy society, but to improve it. Improvement should be what we all want to happen. If these organizations are strong, we all benefit from their efforts. White and Hispanic individuals should also take out memberships in these organizations. This is the right thing to do.

- **Improve educational opportunities.** In the public schools, as well as public institutions of higher learning, all students need to see diversity on all levels, from the teachers to the administrators. Universities need to do a self-examination and come to the conclusion that they need to seriously recruit African Americans for faculty, staff and administrative duties. This will be a big challenge, due to the *pecking* order, but room needs to be made for African Americans.

- **Improve fairness in the criminal justice system.** In many instances, African Americans are viewed by the criminal justice system as the enemy. Therefore, the incarceration rate for African Americans is extremely high. We need to ensure that fairness exists in the system. Blacks should have the same access to diversion programs, alternatives to incarceration, probation and other programs as other violators. Criminal justice personnel should be required to take classes in cultural awareness and human relations. After release programs need to be set up to reintegrate our inmates back into society and their family structure.

- **Greater collaboration between blacks and Hispanics.** Racism has created an atmosphere of competitiveness that has divided the African American and Hispanic communities. In the past, both communities have competed for *what is left*, and both end up with very little. Competition has caused blacks and Hispanics to view each other with suspicion, and our communities have been

> devoid of positive interaction. Racism has impacted both groups, and we are both still being affected by institutional racism. We have common issues and common interests. Blacks and Hispanics need to begin a meaningful dialogue and collaborate to eradicate barriers of inequality. The drop-out rate among black and Hispanic children should be the first issue that we consider, and we should collaborate to develop a mutual strategy to help our children. Keeping our children in school and quality education should be our highest priority. Let the dialogue begin.

If all New Mexicans joined hands, dropped personal agendas and enacted these few initiatives, the condition of African Americans would improve significantly. We have the resources. The question is – *do we have the will*?

Chapter XIII

Yes Lord, Yes!

At an early age, I was taught that when God speaks we must listen. I was brought up in the church; consequently, there has always been a spiritual side of my life. As mentioned in an earlier chapter, I *had* to attend church whether I wanted to or not. Sleeping in on Sunday morning was never an option, Mom saw to that. When I got to college, I proclaimed myself free; I had been liberated out of Hobbs, out of the house, and out of the church. Free at last! Free at last! Little did I realize at that time that just because you are out of the church, church will never be out of you.

Once I left Hobbs and arrived in Albuquerque to attend college, I stopped attending church services. After of couple of months, I began to miss the fellowship that I had enjoyed at Ebenezer Baptist Church in Hobbs, and I would borrow a car from one of my friends and drive to various churches in central Albuquerque. At the first church that I attended I felt out of place because no one spoke to me, nor did they make me feel welcome. I tried another church and the same thing happened. I didn't feel as though I belonged, so I went back to sleeping in on Sunday mornings. After a while, that spiritual side began to tug at me again. I began to attend mass with some of my friends. I would sit while they were kneeling and kneel while they were standing, but I eventually got the routine down and got in sync with everyone else.

After college, I drifted away from the church altogether and was very spiritually unfulfilled. I attended parties on Saturday nights and fished or played golf on Sundays, but these activities did not fill the void in my life. I had a wife, three beautiful children, a good job, lots of friends and a nice home, but I was still running on empty.

In 1976, I met Reverend W. C. Trotter, the pastor of Mt. Olive Baptist Church in Albuquerque, and he invited me to fellowship with his congregation. I told him that I would, but I procrastinated for several weeks, maybe even months, before I actually decided to accept his invitation. When I finally did attend, it was a good spiritual re-connection with my Christian roots. By this time my marriage was failing, and I had prayed that getting back into church would somehow be the answer to our marital problems.

My wife and I ended up going our separate ways, but I rededicated myself to serving the Lord. I became an ordained deacon in the church, and taught the Young Adult Sunday School class. I served as a deacon for just about 7 years.

During this time in my life, I had decided to enter into politics and run for public office. I knew that this would provide a forum for me to change the world. I wanted to be a champion for the poor and introduce legislation that would make things better for the *little guy*. I wanted to open the doors of equal opportunity by standing up and speaking for those who could not speak for themselves. This was *my* plan, but God had a somewhat different road for me to follow, and on December 10, 1978, He called me to the ministry.

I did not want to go into the ministry, I wanted to follow my plans to go into politics and change the world. My mind was set and my plans had been laid. It was either my way or God's way. I had to learn the hard way, but I learned that God never loses an argument. I avoided God's calling on my life for five years, trying to do things my way. What a mess! But there really is only one way - God's Way.

On my father's side of the family the roots of Christian service runs deep. My grandfather was the pastor of a Baptist church in

Clarksville, Texas. I had two aunts that entered the ministry, and before he passed, my father accepted his call and began to preach sermons at the church where he attended while they were without a pastor. On my mother's side, I have uncles and cousins who have entered into Christian service. In fact, my mother has been the Superintendent of the Sunday School at Ebenezer Baptist Church for over fifty years.

In August of 1986, I was ordained as a minister of the gospel by Reverend F. W. Wells, and I have never had any regrets about that decision. I have pledged the rest of my life to serving the Lord. Shortly after being ordained, Reverend Trotter passed, and I was later called to pastor the Mt. Olive Baptist Church. Many of my friends that I used to hang out with shook their heads in disbelief that I would become a minister. Sixteen years later, some are still shaking their heads, but I know that I have to please God and not man.

I was the pastor of the Mt. Olive Baptist Church for approximately five years. The church could not pay enough to sustain my family, and I was not able to find another job in New Mexico to supplement my income, so I resigned my pastorate and accepted a job at San Joaquin Delta College as the Director of Affirmative Action. My plan was to find a church once I was in California. At the college I had a great salary, a nice office, a fantastic condo, and a new start. Three months later, the Lord spoke to my heart and directed me to return to Albuquerque. I ignored what God was saying to me and I continued to enjoy the *good* life in California.

Around 3:00 P.M. one afternoon, I was on my way from Stockton to Sacramento, and I fell asleep at the wheel of the car that I was driving. I was traveling north at about 70 miles per hour, and *I fell asleep.* The car veered to the right. There was some loose gravel and a bunch of sunflowers on the side of the road. When the car hit the shoulder of the road, the noise from the gravel hitting against the underside of the car woke me up just in time to avoid a serious accident. If I had veered to the left, I would not be writing these words today. The traffic in the southbound lane was quite heavy, and not only I, but also others, could have been hurt or even killed. I stopped the car and got out. My legs began to shake and I observed the cloud of dust behind me. A lady stopped and asked me if I was okay. I could hardly speak, but I managed to say, *Thank you.*

When I got back to Stockton, I went into prayer and I accepted the fact that God was directing me back to Albuquerque. I knew that God had something for me to do, but I didn't know exactly what. The next day, I resigned my position. I called a friend of mine, and he flew out and helped me pack my belongings, and I moved back to Albuquerque. I had no church, no job, and no place to stay, but as soon as I returned I realized that God had already worked those things out.

Another friend of mine was in the process of moving to Washington, D.C. and I moved into his place. That took care of one problem, and I trusted in the Lord for the other needs. I knew that if I was obedient to Him, I had nothing to worry about.

I continued to pray and ask God to show me what He wanted me to do. I wanted to know why I was back in Albuquerque. In the middle of the night, the Lord spoke to my heart again. *Build me a church in Rio Rancho.* My immediate reaction was *Rio Rancho?* I knew very little about Rio Rancho, New Mexico. I thought that this was a place where New Yorkers congregated and it was a big wasteland. I drove out to Rio Rancho, looked around, and asked, *Why*?

I organized a committee of people that lived in the area and sought help from the Missions Division of the Baptist Convention of New Mexico. We named the church Emmanuel Missionary Baptist Church and opened our doors in August of 1993. Our first meeting place was in a shopping center. When the time came to renew our lease, the management company decided not to renew because they wanted to lease space in the same shopping center to an enterprise that would be serving liquor. We were given 30 days to vacate the building. Within a few months, the management company leased the same space to another church. I often wonder if the decision to move our church out was a racial decision, since the new church was a white congregation. We found space in another shopping center, and were able to continue our services without interruption.

My instructions from the Lord had been to *build a church,* not to lease space in a shopping center, so we began to look for some land on which to build. We found some land, and some was donated, and within a couple of years, we built a church edifice with a sanctuary, offices, classrooms, and a kitchen. We recently completed an addition to our existing building. I know that this is what God had for me to do, and I learned that obedience to His will does pay off. To God be the glory! Through this experience I learned a very valuable lesson in regards to obedience. God speaks to the heart and we must act through faith and obey. God honors faith and obedience.

I have no regrets about going into the ministry. I have had my ups and downs, but when I balance the scale, there have been more ups. Nothing could be more rewarding than the work that we have done to help shape the lives of the children in our church. I hold the children and their parents accountable for academic achievement. I *personally* review every report card of every child in our church, including the college students. If a child is not doing well, I meet with the student and the parents, and we work out an improvement plan. We always work on the principle that we believe praise and recognition will help the children to succeed. We give out certificates in recognition of accomplishments, and verbal praise is given to the children and the parents. As a result, I have seen achievement levels rise. We do not accept excuses for low achievement because we expect our children to accept responsibility for the choices they make.

In the ten years that I have been at Emmanuel, we have not lost one child to drugs, alcohol, teenage pregnancy, dropping out of school, being expelled from school, running away from home or being locked up. We have experienced a couple of suspensions, and one detention due to a false accusation that was later cleared up. We are proud of the work we have done with the children of our church. When our youth graduate, they usually go on to college or a technical vocational school. They not only do well - they excel. To God be the glory!

The downs and disappointments that I have had during my years in ministry can be attributed to the meanness that can be found among church people. Unfortunately, this is common in many churches throughout the United States. I can handle the discretions that Christians engage in because they will usually repent and are restored. But meanness that has been deliberately inflicted by one person onto another has been difficult for me to deal with. Evil intent that harms another person's reputation and wellbeing is hard for me to understand, and it causes me great pain when I see it happen. I know that it happens in the secular world, but I am dismayed when it happens in God's church.

I have always tried to live my life according to several learned Biblical principles that have guided me for a long time. These principles include:

#1: **Always treat people right.** Be fair and respectful towards others, even when they are being disrespectful towards you. In all your dealings with other people, always respect their dignity because this may be the only thing that they are holding on to. When you take away a person's dignity, you also take away their humanity. Keep your commitments, and above all, keep your word. If people are dependent on you, do not let them down.

#2: **Always do your best.** This should be a contract that a person makes with him/herself. When a person does their best, regardless of the outcome, no matter what the score, there can be no *losers*. When a person does less than their best, he/she becomes known as a slothful person or a *slacker*. When you do your best, you can look in the mirror and say, *I did not short change anything or anybody.* Then, you hold yourself accountable.

#3: **Tell the truth and shame the devil**. This is a statement that I heard from an elderly person many years ago. When we tell the truth, we also honor God. A lie only gives the devil a stronger foothold in our lives. He bursts with pride when a lie is told because he thrives on lies and deception. A lie is one point in the win column for the devil, but the truth puts him to shame. I have discovered that when one lie is told, another one usually follows to cover the first lie.

#4: **Make a contribution to your community**. Leave things a little better than you found them, and always leave more in than you take out. If we take more out of life than we contribute, we become *takers.* I believe in the principle of reciprocity. In order to get something back, you have to put something in. In each encounter that we have with other people, we either added to their lives or we diminished them in some way. In all things, at all times, keep a positive attitude. A motto that I give to the children in the church is, *Your attitude determines your altitude.* How far we go in life is determined by the attitude that we display.

#5: **Don't complain.** No one appreciates a *whiner.* Don't expect sympathy or expect others to appreciate you, or even like you. When we feel unappreciated, we have a tendency to have a *pity party.* I have found that you don't have to do something, or say something to someone else for him/her to dislike you. Just being who you are can cause some people to dislike you. We can expend a lot of time and energy feeling sorry for ourselves. This can cause us to complain. Instead, we should take everything to the Lord in prayer. Romans 8:28 tells us, *And we know that all things work together for good to them that love God, to them who are the called according to his purpose.*

#6: **Help others along life's journey**. Stand up for the little guy. Speak up for those who cannot speak for themselves. Scripture tells us that *the strong must bear the infirmities of the weak.* It should not matter if that person likes you, or whether he/she has harmed you in the past, *need* should be the pre-requisite for extending help, rather than emotions. After you help someone, don't expect any *high fives*, in fact, the very people that you help may turn on you. However, if they need help in the future, *help them again*. Also, never get beyond saying, *I apologize,* or *I was wrong.*

#7: **Always trust in God.** Trust Him for everything. Proverbs 3:5 says, *Trust in the Lord with all thine heart and lean not unto thine own understanding.* Some battles are not worth fighting. Sometimes we just need to walk away from a fight and leave it in the hands of the Lord. It has been my faith and my trust in God that has helped me through the tough times. Without God's help, I could not have faced the discrimination and racism that came my way growing up black in New Mexico. Things have not changed much for African Americans in today's society.

#8: **Stay positive and don't live in the past.** One of the lessons that I have learned is to avoid living in the past. When one lives in the past, people and/or events from the past still control you. Living in the past will lead one to make excuses, or make one want to seek revenge. Either impulse is destructive and emotionally draining. One of the most liberating experiences that one can have is to let go of something from the past. Old sayings tell us, *Don't cry over spilt milk. You can't put it back in the bottle,* and *You can't unscramble an egg.* Growing up, I did not have a lot of advantages, but I could never use that as an excuse. If I did, then I would be controlled by the past. As mentioned before, I grew up in a racially oppressive environment, but I can't let the negative acts of oppression, racial slurs or discrimination control my conduct today. The past belongs exactly where it is - in the past.

As I continue in my ministry, I realize that God has much more for me to do. It has not been easy, nor is the work getting any easier, but as I walk with the Lord I know that *I can do all things through Christ which strengthens me.* (Philippians 4:13) When I come to the end of my journey and my eulogy is written, all I want said is, *Here lies a servant of God.*

Epilogue

Growing up in New Mexico placed me in an atmosphere where racism was a way of life. Growing up in such an environment and being African American gave me three options. First, I could accept things the way they were, along with all of the humiliation and indignities that were a part of the racial climate. Second, I could become bitter and be consumed by bitterness. Or third, I could work hard to overcome obstacles and not become a victim, but a victor. I chose the latter option.

I cannot truthfully say that I never became bitter; I had my moments. I found that bitterness created no advantage and actually worked against me. Do we turn our heads and ignore what is happening to us? Or do we try to change it and make things better? I have always felt that if there is no challenge, there will be no change. Continued racism in our diverse society should be unacceptable. Discrimination should be a thing of the past. We should not only find acts of discrimination appalling, but disgusting.

We have to ask the questions, **why do African Americans have such a difficult time being accepted in New Mexico? Why are**

there no African Americans on the Governor's Cabinet? Why is there not one African American holding a position as a member of the Board of Regents at any university in the state? Why are there no African American university presidents, vice presidents, and only one high level administrator in the entire state? Why are there no African Americans in upper level administrative positions in the Albuquerque Public Schools, the Rio Rancho Public Schools or The Technical Vocational Institute (TVI)? These are all *public* institutions!

I would suspect that the banks where we have checking and savings accounts, and can't get loans, don't fare any better. We, African Americans, do our banking and purchase cars at places that won't hire us. We eat in restaurants and buy groceries at places that discriminate in their hiring. We donate to non-profit organizations that won't provide services to our people. Even many programs and organizations that receive federal funding exclude blacks.

The black leadership in this state needs to redefine its political strategy. Too often, our leadership has sought to accommodate rather than change. They have sought favors rather than demanding what is rightfully ours. When programs or policies are implemented that provide relief for African Americans, it is looked upon as a *favor* that we should be eternally grateful for receiving. We are expected to praise the grantor at every banquet and every meeting, and in return we get a pat on the head and are turned loose to control on our own people on their behalf.

In many cases, our black leadership is chosen for us. Now is the time to let the established leadership know that there are other voices out there that should be heard, or there will someday be a rude awakening at the polls.

We have heard and trusted the promises made by politicians, but once they are elected they develop *selective* amnesia. (They lied.) When questioned, their response is, *I don't remember saying that.* They promise that we will be invited to the banquet. When the invitations are sent, we show up and sit at the table, but when the meal is served we are given an empty plate. Just because we sit at the table does not make us a diner. After the meal is served, all the top positions are filled and we get what is left. Where I come from, these are called *crumbs.* African Americans have to stop settling for *crumbs and push for a full course meal.* Our black leadership has to not only push for a place at the table, but for a meal on the plate. If we demand our place at the table and we challenge the system, then and only then, will change occur.

The dream of Dr. Martin Luther King, Jr. has not been realized. One of the main reasons for this is that the majority has not stepped up to the plate and said to their fellow majority members, *Enough is enough!* Not everyone is able to challenge the system vocally. This takes a great deal of courage and one's livelihood can be placed in jeopardy. However, each person must find his or her own rhythm – his or her own drumbeat. To march to someone else's drumbeat makes you a puppet, and a puppet has never changed the world. World changers are those who march to the beat that they hear for themselves; that beat that says, dignity for all people. World changers rise to the challenge. There is nothing more liberating than a puppet that breaks rank and chooses to be a puppet no longer. When a puppet becomes a world changer, change really occurs. *No challenge, no change*!

About the Author

Charles E. Becknell is an author, educator, experienced manager, poet, and an ordained minister. He earned Bachelor and Master degrees in Education and a Ph.D. in American Studies, and has taught in the public schools and on the college and university levels.

Dr. Becknell grew up in rural southeastern New Mexico and attended a segregated school until 1954. He obtained a basketball scholarship to the College of St. Joseph (University of Albuquerque) where he became Captain of the basketball team, Secretary of his senior class and President of the Letterman's Club.

After receiving his B.S. in Education, and his M.A. in Secondary Education, Dr. Becknell received a Ford Foundation Fellowship under the Leadership Development Program. He then served an internship at Duke University in Durham, NC, under the Education Improvement Program and began his doctoral studies at Columbia University in New York City.

Dr. Becknell founded and directed the Afro-American Studies Program at the University of New Mexico and held the faculty rank of Assistant Professor. In 1975, at the request of Governor Jerry Apodaca, he accepted a position as Cabinet Secretary for Criminal Justice for the State of New Mexico.

After leaving a distinguished career in State Government, Dr. Becknell worked for one year as a Corporate Executive for a major utility in Albuquerque.

Armed with knowledge and experience from both the public and private sector, Dr. Becknell formed his own company, Becknell & Associates, Inc., a training and human development company. He has conducted numerous workshops and seminars, and given speeches throughout the United States, Puerto Rico, the U. S. Virgin Islands, and West Africa. Dr. Becknell is an excellent motivational speaker, and brings compassion and understanding to the topicshe addresses.

In addition to owning his own consulting firm, Dr. Becknell is the former pastor of Mt. Olive Baptist Church in Albuquerque, New Mexico, the current pastor of Emmanuel Missionary Baptist Church in Rio Rancho, New Mexico, and is a member of numerous civic, religious and community-

oriented organizations. Dr. Becknell is the past Director of Personnel Services for the City of Albuquerque and is extremely knowledgeable about changing trends in today's workforce and what skills managers and supervisors need to become successful in the future.

In addition to this book, Dr. Becknell is the author of *Black Culture in America, Blacks in the Workforce,* and *Expression: A Collection of Poems by Dr. Charles E. Becknell.* He has writen several articles and has appeared on local TV on numerous occasions.

Dr. Becknell is currently on the staff at the University of California at Davis, Extension where he received the Service Excellence Award for excellence in teaching and outstanding service in the field of continuing education.

No Challenge, No Change Order Form

Use this convenient order form to order additional copies of
No Challenge, No Change

Please Print:

Name______________________________

Address______________________________

City____________________ **State**__________

Zip____________________

Phone(   )______________________________

______copies of book @ $**_15.95_** each	$________
NM residents add **$1.00** tax for each book	$________
Postage and handling	$ 3.00
Total amount enclosed	$________

Make checks payable to Jubilee Publications

Send to: **Jubilee Publications**
P.O. Box 15971
Rio Rancho, NM 87174-5971